LANDSCAPES OF THE INTERIOR

"A rare moment when I discover someone capable of responding with such senstivity to the mystique of the North American continent! Someone who has lived intimately with and thought deeply about the mountains and forests and rivers and wildlife of this continent. Someone with the intellectual culture, the scientific knowledge, and the writing skills for conveying this experience to those of us less intimate with this continent in its native grandeur. Don Gayton deserves a place along with the finest of our nature writers.

Such writing as this has inestimable value in this historical moment; for the wilderness world of this continent is one of the last regions of the planet to come under the oppressive influence of the urban literate civilizational traditions. It still survives as an awesome presence constantly transforming itself within the ever-renewing processes of the natural world. The inner world of the human, our song and dance, our sense of the sacred, our deepest aesthetic, emotional, intellectual experiences are evoked by our experiences of the entrancing as well as the foreboding qualities of the natural world. As we lose the pristine presence of this world about us we will depend to an increasing degree upon such writings as these that forever enshrine in our imagination and emotions these impressions of beauty and wonder beyond all understanding."

— Thomas Berry, author of *The Dream of the Earth*

"*Landscapes of the Interior* fills a gap in the ever-burgeoning literature about the western North American landscape. I get tired of the 'macho' West most men write about, and Don Gayton spares us this annoyance. The combination of Don's scientific knowledge and his poet's eye – each of which he uses to inform the other – is unique. He gives us a new place to start, and new tools to use, in our contemplation of the thorny problem of the human relationship with nature. Forcing us to probe deep inside ourselves, he ponders the effect of particular landscapes on humans, the merits of our ecoystem management, and the very question of what dream of Nature it is that we labor under, whether we recognize that dream or not.

Don Gayton asks, "Can we sustain ourselves long enough to sort out our relationship with Nature and find a useful middle ground between science and the mystical?" His scrupulous, sometimes amusing and far-reaching attempts to answer this question are the engaging material of these essays."
— Sharon Butala, author of
The Perfection of the Morning

"This, folks, is *real* literature! *Landscapes of the Interior* is sensuous, precise and instructive; a consummate work of reinhabitory essay. Alive with insight, vivid detail, and astute observation, Gayton's writing deftly and concretely engages a number of the most consequential questions of ecological theory and practice under discussion today. Learned, graceful, intimate and good-natured, *Landscapes of the Interior* evokes a fulsome sense of participation in the deep exploration it chronicles so cleanly. A book not to be missed!"
— Stephanie Mills, author of *In Service of the Wild: Restoring and Reinhabiting Damaged Land*

LANDSCAPES of the INTERIOR

LANDSCAPES of the INTERIOR

Re-Explorations of Nature and the Human Spirit

Don Gayton

NEW SOCIETY PUBLISHERS

<u>Canadian Cataloguing in Publication Data:</u>
Gayton, Don, 1946 -
Landscapes of the interior

Includes bibliographical references.
ISBN 1-55092-284-X (bound) -- ISBN 1-55092-285-8 (pbk.)
1. Landscape -- Canada, Western. 2. Landscape -- West (U.S.)
3. Philosophy of nature. 4. Nature (Aesthetics). I. Title.
FC3205.4.G39 1996   917.1204'3   C96-910222-4
F1060.G39 1996

Cover design by Val Speidel from photographs
by Jim Romo and the author.

Printed in Canada on acid-free, partially recycled
(20 percent post-consumer) paper using soy-based inks
by Best Book Manufacturers.

Portions of this book have previously appeared in the following
publications: "The Mountain Electric" in *The Trumpeter*; "Cowboy
Fiction" in *Books in Canada*; "Tallgrass Dream" in *Canadian
Geographic;* and "Visions of Methuselah" in *The Kootenay Review.*

The author gratefully acknowledges the editorial assistance and
encouragement offered by Martha Gould, Ronald Hatch,
Chris Plant and Tom Wayman.

Inquiries regarding requests to reprint all or part of *Landscapes of
the Interior* should be addressed to New Society Publishers
at the address below.

Canada ISBN: 1-55092-285-8 (Paperback)
Canada ISBN: 1-55092-284-X (Hardback)
U.S.A. ISBN: 0-86571-344-8 (Paperback)
U.S.A. ISBN: 0-86571-343-X (Hardback)

To order directly from the publishers, please add $3.00 to the price of
the first copy, and $1.00 for each additional copy
(plus GST in Canada). Send check or money order to:

New Society Publishers,
P.O. Box 189, Gabriola Island, BC V0R 1X0, Canada.

Contents

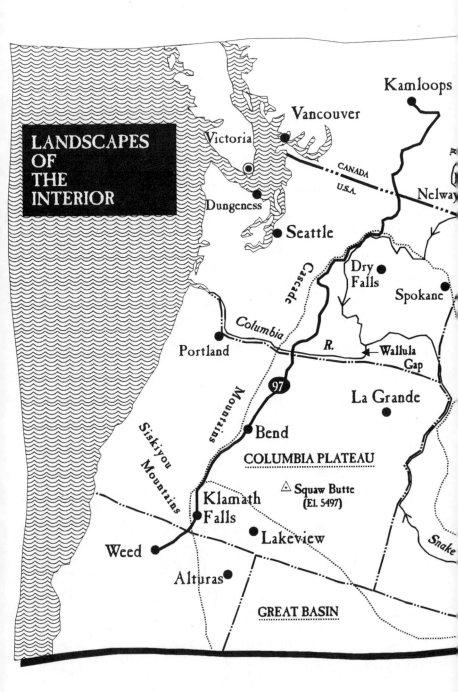

LANDSCAPES OF THE INTERIOR

Kamloops

Vancouver

Victoria

CANADA

U.S.A.

Nelway

Dungeness

Seattle

Cascade

Dry Falls

Spokane

Columbia

Portland

R.

Wallula Gap

97

La Grande

Mountains

Siskiyou Mountains

Bend

COLUMBIA PLATEAU

△ Squaw Butte (El. 5497)

Klamath Falls

Lakeview

Snake

Weed

Alturas

GREAT BASIN

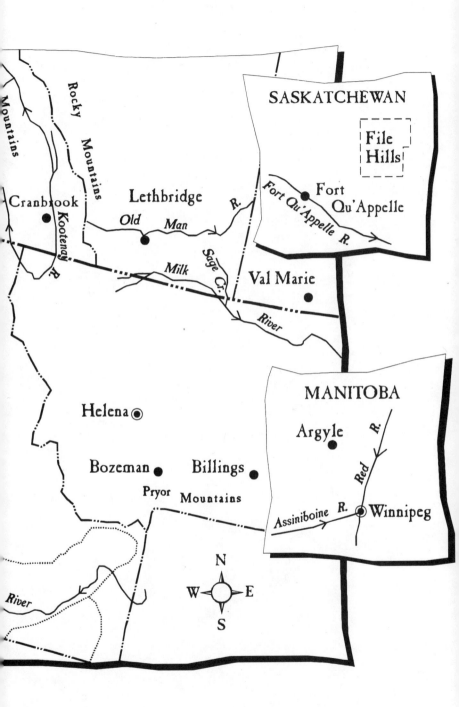

1

The Mountain Electric

I SET A FAST PACE UP THE TRAIL, walking towards a first night in the mountains of southeastern British Columbia. My small pack rode too lightly and I found myself wishing for the greasy and pleasant fatigue of a three- or four-day hike. The trail gained altitude steadily, making a series of switchbacks along the lower flanks of the massive Kokanee Ridge. I was still in timber, but occasionally the footpath crossed open and brushy avalanche chutes, and from these I could see that tree-line was not far above me. Downslope on my left lay the creek, hidden by the trees but plainly audible when I stopped to listen. Beyond the creek and sweeping upward again was the parallel twin of the ridge I was on, its naked granite peaks now fawn colored in the late summer sunlight. Far up ahead of me these two parallel ridges converged, and my destination was the high, level saddle that lay at the center of that convergence.

The trail, having gained altitude and momentum through the switchbacks, now carried straight upward along the flank, on gradually moderating ground. I passed the rusted trucks of an old ore cart, artifact of a brief heyday of silver mining. Somewhere up above me lay the foundations of the Molly Gibson mine bunkhouse, which was carried down the mountain by a massive snow avalanche on Christmas eve of 1902, killing nine miners. Death by snow avalanche — not all that uncommon here — is known locally as "the big ride."

During my first winter living in Nelson I learned what I could about this ridge, talking to people who knew it and reading descriptions in local hiking guides. From certain parts of town you could just see its elongated, jagged comb, looming above the mountains around it. The ridge often caught me by surprise, as if it were watching me. People said winter storms brewed on its slopes, and the glacier on its north side meant the water in the Kokanee drainage stayed cold right through summer. I bought a 1:50,000-scale topographical map and soon became mesmerized by the tiny, convoluted lines that projected the ridge's tortured faults and outcrops on to paper. This hastily arranged summer trip to the Kokanee Ridge was the first of my re-explorations of natural landscapes. For years I travelled simply to experience places, some wild, some domesticated, some forgotten. Now I would travel to discover what compelled me to seek these places out, and to understand this long-standing, sometimes obsessive transaction between landscape and myself.

My re-exploration had a larger context beyond the personal. The great age of primary exploration — of finding and recording new places — is over, and we are now firmly in an age of re-exploration, where we may discover the mechanics, the meanings and the essences of those found places.

The natural landscapes of my primary fascination lie between the West Coast and Wallace Stegner's Hundredth Meridian, a west of a certain dryness, and of space. As an immigrant, I can also lay claim to the interior regions in the West of both Canada and the United States. I hoped in my re-exploration to go beyond simply looking again, to begin finding tiny grains of constancy in these diverse landscapes, bits of natural truth. The writer Barry Lopez says that stories originate in the difference between the inner landscape and the outer one. I wanted to prove him right.

The heavy new hiking boots I wore had a resolute air about them. The stiffness that seemed so pointless in the sporting goods store began to make sense as the trail gradually turned from duff to rock. I had the definite sense of a beginning of some kind. As I gained altitude, the trees became short and stunted, many of them showing bright exposures of new wood, where snow avalanches had sheared off their tops. The barren avalanche chutes that coursed downslope through the timber were becoming more and more common as I climbed higher, and finally, the individual chutes merged to become a single avalanche field. In the midst of this steep and shattered landscape, a teardrop-shaped grove of mature Engelmann spruce stood by itself, having somehow gained the stature to withstand the awesome power of moving sheets of snow. I realized that tree-line on this landscape was not determined by altitude, but rather by rock angle and avalanche frequency.

Landscape. It is a curious one, this term that I use so often, this focus of my re-exploration. Profoundly human-centered, the "scape" in landscape means view, *our* view. We use the word extensively in art and photography, and even use it to describe the orientation of paper. The word has become hackneyed with overuse by developers, who will call a few pathetic shrubs "landscaping," and soiled by bureaucrats, who refer to "administrative landscapes." In almost every case, the word "arrangement" can be substituted for the word landscape, since that seems to be the quality we look for. Yet in spite of our bastard uses of the word, I sense that "landscape" does have an existence totally outside our own self-serving definition of it. This much I did know, at the outset of my re-exploration: there is a subtle coherency and trueness to the way nature arranges its objects in space, and its trees on this mountain ridge. What I was not so sure of is whether we can restore those qualities to a natural landscape once we have degraded it, and whether our own domesticated landscapes can ever achieve their own trueness and coherency.

Giving voice to landscape will be a difficulty. Describing this mountain ridge demands a poet's unbridled, spiritual view, but some of the ridge's finest processes and secrets must first be teased out, investigated, and understood, before being open to that lyric view. The science I use to do this though, will demand dissection into components, classification, and a certain passivity and precision of language. Whether the spruces in the grove are *Picea glauca engelmannii* or *Picea glauca glauca* will be important to me as a scientific investigator, but my actual experience of these grey-barked and elegant trees can become deeply buried under category and language. As a scientist I must tuck the identified trees into certain age and cover classes, and then go on to analyse the grove itself as having a low interior-to-edge ratio, a feature common in disturbed habitats. Component categories like these are dangerous, of course, since they are the deductive and isolated parts severed from an organic whole. The improbable beauty of a spruce grove in an avalanche field may easily be lost in the standard deviation of one of its mechanisms, yet an understanding of the grove's many mechanisms also produces insights of improbable beauty. For my re-exploration to be successful, I will have to engage both the lyric and the scientific, find a balance between them, and make their languages work together.

This mountain I am on still reeks of glaciers, of destruction, of late Pleistocene inevitabilities. There were times during that distant era when the ice lay four thousand feet thick in the valleys. Peaks of the higher mountains became nunataks, unglaciated plant refuges, that provided some of the first seeds to recolonize the barren and scoured ground after the ice disappeared. Most of the plants that populate this trailside — Indian paintbrush, fireweed, glacier lilies — probably owe their existence to the peaks far above them. A few seeds may also have actually survived under the ice in the valleys. Canadian ecologist E.C. Pielou describes finding 10,000-year-old seeds of the arctic lupine plant in fossil lemming nests in the Yukon. Given moisture and warmth, the seeds broke ten millennia of dormancy and promptly germinated. I would definitely be a lyrical ex-scientist, were it not for information like this.

The trail rose through one last, steep switchback before it reached the saddle. Again I wished this hike had consumed more time and effort, so as to increase the drama of my arrival. As it was, I was only a few hours away from home and office. I climbed very deliberately over the last few feet of trail, trying to substitute concentration for time, and then finally stepped out onto the open saddle. Here was lithosphere: the world of rock. I stood between the two jagged, electric ridges, two continuous fractures of granite. Loose and broken rock was strewn everywhere across the saddle. When would all this shattering of ridge rock have occurred? I had visions of night-time eruptions, when shards of tensioned granite exploded off their mother slabs, like popcorn off a griddle.

This was the same landscape I had flown over many times before, a prairie person looking down on the snowbound and fractalled eternity of southern British Columbia's Rockies, Purcells, Selkirks and Monashees, from 20,000 feet up. Now I sensed instinctively that I was seeing this landscape from just the right elevation. These summits were remnants of an original land surface, and everything else had been ground down in the maws of giant cirque and valley glaciers. I stood on the absolute reciprocal of prairie.

These two ridges and their saddle were born in an orogeny, an upward buckling of British Columbia's crust when some broken and errant plate of earth crashed against its ancient coastline. In the beginning, after the orogeny, there was nothing on the scalded rocks of this Selkirk Range to take away from their absolute lithic purity: it was the primary landscape. But even from that first day, these ridges began to act out their internal and constant logic of erosion, from solid slab to broken rock, from broken rock to pebbles, pebbles to sand, and from sand, ultimately, to clay. And magic clay, with its ability to hold moisture, and its electrical charges that attract and hold the ions that are plant nutrients, becomes the foundation of soil. Movement downslope continues, in boisterous rockfalls and airborne glitter of granite dust. Somewhere below the peak, lithosphere surrenders dominance to biosphere, to elegant bluebells and whistling marmots. Life on earth might have begun amongst a marine soup of complex molecules, but *terrestrial* life could be said to begin when sand turns to clay.

The nervous energy that had propelled me up the trail's switchbacks was still with me. It was getting dark and I was alone on a mountain, so I turned my attention to finding a place to camp. A few hundred yards farther onto the saddle I saw a small lake ahead, a lovely mons cupped between the two converging ridges. I left the trail and found a level spot for the tent, almost a promontory above the lake, that was carpeted with elk sedge and moss. For the next twenty minutes I busied myself arranging lantern, tent and sleeping bag, creating an odd little island of domesticity amongst a sea of rock. Setting up a wilderness camp is like going through a lab experiment in the hierarchy of needs: shelter, food, heat, light. My concentration, in rapidly fading daylight, was total. Finally I sat down in front of the erected tent, and the tension of the last several hours released. An unexpected, curious wave of emotion passed through me. I saw now that I had unwittingly chosen a campsite in the center of a magnificent twilight amphitheatre. In front of me, amidst the rock rubble, lay a lake of darkening indigo glass. The two ridges that buttressed each side were still phosphorescing from departed sun, while the sky darkened steadily towards pure night. High above, on a vast proscenium arch, rode Venus and the great, wheeling moon. A sudden, unexpected spasm caught my breath, held it for a brief, revealing moment, and then passed. For the next few minutes I wept, uncontrollably, until a deep internal well-spring I had never known or acknowledged was finally, and profoundly, emptied.

It was now fully dark and I lit a small camping lantern I had brought with me. I noticed a slight tremble as I held the wooden match against the asbestos mantle, a residue of emotional passage. At the far end of lyrical lay myth, mysticism, epiphany. I had no sense of the lay of those territories. The lantern was new, and probably one-tenth the weight of the one my father used to lug around on our family camping trips, but the familiar hiss of white gas as it hit the glowing mantle had not changed over the years. I slid my bag and sleeping pad towards the open tent flap until I could see the night sky. I knew I would not sleep well that night, but right then, in spite of a hundred uncertainties, I felt profoundly comfortable. Above my head were the reassuring, lantern-lit walls of the tent, and out past the tent flap, beyond the tiny pool of lantern light, lay a dormant landscape and a blazing universe.

The little lantern hissed pleasantly. There was something

about its temporary and consumptive overbrightness that was like night-time consciousness itself. James Agee wrote *Let Us Now Praise Famous Men* at night, with aid of a kerosene lamp, a lamp whose light was similar to this one. Agee's feverish light would illuminate the bare kitchen table of the southern sharecropper's cabin, and he would write, "All over Alabama the lamps are out." All the lamps of course, except his.

I tried to snuggle further down into my sleeping bag, cursing that anonymous short-limbed, right-handed, average-weight, medium-height individual for whom everything is designed. In the end, I put my jacket over my shoulders, and was grateful for the warm night. The familiar hiss of the lantern was fading gradually, as was its light. Instead of pumping it up again or shutting it off, I decided to let the flame slowly exhaust itself.

I slept fitfully, disturbed by my experience and unused to the demands of a narrow sleeping bag and slippery mattress pad. My tent was a tiny, excessively human satellite drifting amongst rock and stars. The air on the mountain was absolutely still, and the silence was eerie. As I twisted and turned in my bag, I thought I heard human voices in the distance. I had absolutely no desire to see anyone, wanting to let my little satellite drift alone into new territory. Then I heard the sound of a car engine, and shortly after that, the sound of the little bells local hikers use for alerting bears. Finally I realized my consciousness was so disturbed by the lack of background noise that it was writing these audible notes itself, and beaming them out against the textured night silence.

Sunrise the next morning was like a revealed secret. Getting on with its hundred-thousandth, its millionth morning, the Kokanee Ridge shared its everyday marvels with me totally, without hesitation. I crawled out of the sleeping bag and stood up, feeling disheveled in my underwear and tangled beard, in the face of such alpine perfection. Exploratory morning light fingered its way through the jagged eastern ridgeline, slowly illuminating down the face of the western ridge. Ribbons of mist moved across the windless surface of the lake, drawn forward by some unseen mechanism. Up in the rockfield, a single marmot whistled. The world had emerged new from the chrysalis of night, and was still carefully unfolding itself.

I could see a pattern to the alpine lakes in these mountains. They were all roughly circular, and located just beneath major ridges like this one. A small meadow could be found at the outflow end of the lake, and in the water just in front of the meadow would be a small logjam of dead trees. These trees would have been killed by avalanche, windthrow or lightning, and drifted across the lake to the outflow. There they would patiently wait their turn to rot, turn into peat, and feed the bear grass in the meadow.

I made hobo coffee and ate a granola bar for breakfast, and then sat down to write some notes. The plan for my re-exploration of landscapes was now simple and obvious: I would spiral outward from my newly-adopted mountain community, looping through the Canadian and American interiors, into mountain and prairie, to revisit natural landscapes, to learn how their outlines alter the way I see and live, to lift their veils by both poetry and science, and to crystallize the insights into words, journals and stories. The re-exploration would be a physical one but also, in the best tradition of exploration, a mental one, into my own thoughts and memories, as well as into the lives and art of others. I knew that my re-exploration would have to be largely a solitary one, since I am so subject to the instinctive practicality of groups, and practical was not what I was after. In solitude my senses are sharper. In solitude I tend to let down the barriers to fugitive and esthetic perception. As a writer, I hoped to harvest the observations of my re-exploration, but some caution about nostalgia would be necessary. When I see a new natural landscape, I experience an immediate sense of personal ownership, followed by nostalgia once I leave it. Nostalgia is wonderful, but it can be the writer's trap.

The original explorers required the skills of endurance for their extended trips; I on the other hand, with a life firmly rooted in the everyday of jobs, family and community, would require the skills of a juggler, and my trips and explorations would be brief, intense forays. I would have to be ready for re-exploration at a moment's notice, since the patterns of my existence are somewhat obscure, even to me. Some re-explorations would be serendipitous and none would be to the Banff or Grand Canyon-type spectacles: I had grown wary of the kind of natural grandiosity that demands nothing of the viewer and everything of the landscape. I knew the re-exploration would take at least a year, perhaps longer; I was prepared to trust my intuition to know when it was over.

A boulder cracked loose on the ridge above me and bounded down the slope, shattering into smaller and smaller pieces as it hit other rocks. The rifle-shot sound of the initial crack echoed back and forth between the ridges long after the shattered rock was still.

It was time to leave, and I began to repack my tent and bag. I knew that in the course of the re-exploration I would have to confront my own persistent unease about the ways we choose to inhabit our landscapes, as well as my own interests in both ecology and resource use, interests that conflict, often painfully. I also hoped the re-exploration would free the concept of landscape from bureaucracies, from developers, and from its painterly, English-countryside connotations, and give the word the boundless, Western Interior potential it deserved. Then there was the matter of the strange, unexpected emotional release of the night before; I knew now that if I were to truly understand landscape, I would have to explore the unknown springs from which those feelings came.

☉

2

Canyon

I HAD A RITUAL FOR MY VISITS to that deep and narrow canyon. At the end of the walk up from the ranch, I would stop short of the mouth, to wait and collect a few sticks for the fire. After a few moments I would enter, crossing from plangent afternoon sun to a kind of separate and constant dusk. The canyon's layered rock walls would glow with a faint bluish tinge.

Buck Creek starts somewhere above tree-line, and flows through the canyon all the way down to sagebrush. Originally the creek ran parallel to the main river, but sometime in the distant Pleistocene it turned abruptly, confronting a massive sandstone ridge that separated the two. The result of that unrecorded confrontation was a narrow, vertical canyon cut through bedded sandstone, and a contented Buck, now joined with its central drainage. Whatever violence that had accompanied the creation of this tiny canyon was resolved in total peace. Even during spring flood the Buck flowed like silk down its smooth and rounded bed.

Just inside the canyon entrance, the sandstone walls widened out to form a circular plunge pool, about twenty feet across. There were four pools in all, one above the other, the first one being the largest. The water in the pools was tea-colored, even though the Buck ran clear both above and below the canyon.

As a dusty young hired man on an Okanagan ranch, this canyon and its water provided retreat and solace at the end of the long workday. After my token wait at the entrance, I would move to the first pool. My work clothes, sticky with hay dust and sweat, would go into a neat pile on the first ledge, next to the sagebrush sticks I had collected. Only then did I slide quietly into the water, to float on my back and look upward. The west wall of this pool was a series of ledges leading up to a sheer sandstone face; the east wall formed a broad, curved overhang, reminiscent of a church nave. Half-way up the west wall a scrappy ponderosa pine had established on a ledge. It presided over the canyon, a modest icon.

After a few minutes in the first pool I would climb the narrow sandstone spillway to the second pool, float for a time, then go to the third and finally the fourth. Sometimes I felt suspended, as if I were floating through the rooms of a fantastic sculpture gallery, each one a different statement of color, texture and form.

After my swim, I would return to the ledge of the first pool to build a tiny fire from the gnarled and twisted sagebrush sticks, and drink from a canteen. Pungent sage smoke would curl straight upward on its way out of the windless canyon.

The rancher I worked for was an old man in those days, and is long since dead. At the time I saw him only as a kind of grim co-ordinator of cattle, grass and barbwire, but later on I realized he must have known of the very personal, mystical nature of the canyon. That would explain his casual, well-timed remark about "those pools on the Buck, up above Bigsage Pasture," for the benefit of one he must have known would seek them out and then promptly deny anyone else's presence there. Certainly it was not long before the water of that canyon flowed only for me.

For years I thought about revisiting the place. In my experience of natural landscapes, the canyon stood out in my memory as one of the more openly spiritual places, rising above the level of simple nostalgia. Buck Creek was prominent on my itinerary for re-exploration.

Memory, however, can be vindictive, contemplating change with bitterness and anger. It was the potato chip, balanced on the first ledge like some obscenely alien butterfly, that first caught my eye. The chip, a nearby paper plate, and several large, garish graffiti now lay strewn across a personal tapestry of my own memory, one that had lain inviolate for twenty-five years. The graffiti were spray-painted in orange Dayglo on the sandstone overhang of the first pool. "FERG 89" and "TORCHY," they screamed. There were a few other initials as well; "B.D." was one. The authors would be high school graduates desperate to enhance personal identities by hijacking the spirit of the place.

My long-awaited reunion with the canyon destroyed, I stopped only long enough to survey the litter and the damage. A cold wind passed through my guts and I felt as if I had come home to a break-in. I left cleanly, not wanting to waste time in useless rage.

I was well into the long, furious walk back down through the pasture when anger finally gave way to duty, and to the service of memory.

First I built a fire on the rock ledge, reversing the old ritual, and immolated the potato chip, the plate, and some bits of candy wrapper. Then I stripped, waded into the first pool, took a handful of gritty sand from the bottom, and began to scrub the graffiti off the sandstone wall. It was slow work. A handful of sand would last only a few strokes before slipping through my fingers. I had brought nothing with me, so I put my socks over my hands, to better hold the sand.

Parts of the sandstone were deeply stained by the paint. I scraped those areas with the sharp edge of a stone, and then feathered the slight depressions back by scrubbing with more sand. It seemed appropriate to remove the graffiti from this place with primitive technology.

Resting once or twice, I lay back into the water and into the significant memory I was trying to repair. It was here, in the first pool of Buck Creek canyon, that my future wife and I saw each other naked for the first time. Brown water flowed over white bodies, sand gradually sifted over and covered our feet, and the luminous sandstone somehow softened the enormity of those first moments. Spirit, flesh, naked and humble: the meeting was a human use of natural landscape that was as valid as a mountain, as legitimate as a tree.

The very fragility of the sandstone was an asset to my work. I was able to scrape deeply enough into the body of the wall that I could get beyond the paint's deepest penetration. I could train my memory to accept change, since change is a dynamic of nature, but I would never let it accept degradation.

Before visiting the canyon, I had stopped in to see the rancher's son. He was a little older than I; in the early days we had talked about becoming partners on the ranch. He warned me about the state of the canyon, and said that some aboriginal rock art farther down the valley had recently been defaced by people who had chipped their own initials right into the figures. A comparison of aboriginal rock art with graffiti crossed my mind momentarily, but I dropped it. Rock art and nature were not derivative; they came from within themselves and had no need to parasitize the purity and sincerity of another's intent.

When the wall was finally finished, I returned to the ledge and dressed. This time, my clothes had none of that fine old stink of hay, sweat and horses. They could still, I mused, if I had stayed on. I could even have guarded this place on grad nights.

As I left, I took a last look up the canyon. The ponderosa pine up on the west wall had prospered, and the place was clean again. Fresh sandstone was evident on the overhang, but no paint could be seen, and I had scrubbed broadly enough that even the shapes of the letters could no longer be made out. I hoped that a few years of weathering would bring the entire wall back to its original grainy blue-white, and memory would then be served.

☉

3

Visions of Scabland

I KNEW THIS HAD TO BE THE RIGHT ROAD; only one paved highway passed through Odessa and I was on it. The photograph in the book showed the rows of massive ripples as they marched through eastern Washington prairie, and the caption underneath said "Three miles E. of Odessa." As soon as I passed the grain elevators at the far edge of town, I checked the odometer in my aging van. All the land to the south of the road was farmed; that was a bad sign. The photograph was dated 1974, documenting a site Bretz had identified on foot fifty years before. What was visible in prairie in the seventies could easily be obliterated in wheatfields now. I hoped desperately that the photo was of the other side of the road, which was still in rough pasture and sagebrush.

Harlen Bretz's massive book lay on the seat beside me, open to the chapter on giant ripple marks. It contained descriptions and modern airphotos of the sites he had located in the 1920s, including the Odessa site. Bretz was a man obsessed with the mysterious Channelled Scabland complex of east-central Washington State. He studied landforms in places like Odessa so much that they finally chose him, and opened their vaulted secrets to him.

Scientific obsessions that run deep enough can slide into lyric realms. Bretz's work was an example of this: it demanded re-exploration. I knew most of the eastern Washington country already, but now I wanted to see it as Bretz had, as a post-flood landscape, to see the ripple marks that were benchmarks for his flood theory, and to participate in the mysteries of the scablands. I hoped also to resolve my quandary about the man himself.

Before the re-exploration, I sat down with Bretz's book together with a good road map of Washington. Some of the sites he identified were near towns that had slid off the map into oblivion, like West Bar and Tokio Station. But one site was near Odessa, a small eastern Washington community that had hung on. I knew the town. The memory of its three or four quiet, tree-lined streets stood apart from the old patina of anger that I had carefully preserved from the Vietnam War days.

Bretz had commented on how difficult it could be to see the ripple marks, and told of ranchers who reacted with surprise when he pointed out ripples on their own land. The Odessa site was to be my only chance at the marks and I realized, as the odometer approached three, that I was desperate to see them.

The road followed the crest of a low rise. At mile 3.2 the ripples suddenly appeared, simple, obvious and suggestive of immense forces. There were perhaps two dozen in formation, running at right angles through the overgrazed pasture. They were rounded, but each crest was skewed forward slightly — skewed downstream, away from the Rockies, towards Portland and the Pacific Ocean. The afternoon sun caught the darker yellow of crested wheatgrass in the troughs between the ripples, highlighting the repeating pattern of crest and trough.

When water flows over loose sand, ripples are created in the sand surface, making a visible mirror of the invisible turbulence of moving water. These ripples were identical to those found in the sand at the bottom of a stream, or on a sandy beach, but on a massively larger scale.

I pulled over, collected Bretz's book, a calculator and my notebook, and left my van unceremoniously in the ditch alongside the road. When I had walked well out onto the crest of one of the ripples, I turned upstream, towards Spokane, and began to pace. My estimate of a yard is gauged by stepping forward until I feel the first twinge in my upper thigh muscles, a fairly reliable indicator. The first chord, the distance from crest through trough to crest, was 80 yards. The next one was 64 yards, the third one 68. I sat down on a ripple crest and opened the book to the "Hydraulics" chapter. Bretz had created a mathematical formula that related ripple chord to the depth of the water that made the ripple, and I plugged my average chord length into his formula. The number staggered me: I did the math a second time before I was satisfied the answer was right. A chill ran up the length of my spine; the ripple I was sitting on was produced by moving water 150 feet deep. If a fourteen-story building sat on this empty prairie 12,500 years ago, all but the penthouse suite would be under water.

I walked back to the van slowly, moving through faint echoes of current. I turned around often, trying to fix the ripples permanently in memory. Then I took a few photographs, just to remind myself how much more the eye and mind can see than the camera.

In 1923, an unknown young geologist proposed an astounding theory. J. Harlen Bretz documented a whole series of erosional landforms in eastern Washington, collectively named them the "Channelled Scablands," and claimed they were all part of a single geological event — a cataclysmic post-glacial flood, that happened 12½ millennia ago. Furthermore, he claimed evidence of the same flood could also be seen in northern Idaho and western Oregon. The scale of his proposed event and the volume of its water put it far beyond biblical proportions; this flood would be the largest in the known history of Earth. He was not believed.

Long before reaching Odessa, my scabland journey had begun as I left Nelson and crossed the British Columbia border into northeastern Washington. Heading southwest, going against the grain of three low mountain ranges, I finally entered the Columbia River valley north of Grand Coulee dam. This was the landscape in which moraine met mesa; where Canadian ice and mountain faulting surrendered dominance to American lava, water and wind. This was landscape on a grand scale, landscape of personal transaction, perhaps even landscape of obsession. As I got closer to the Columbia, I had to pull over and check my bearings and confirm that the river was in fact running *northward* at this point, in a major aberration from its southwesterly flow toward the Pacific. This was the "Big Bend," where the river looped back up towards its origins in Canada before turning southward again on its final run to the Pacific.

I passed by Grand Coulee dam with ambivalent feelings. This dam was the first stake driven through the unsullied heart of the Columbia River, but it was also a beacon of work and hope for thousands of men during the Depression. My father was one of those men: he still loves to tell stories of the work camps and the excitement. My favorite of those stories is how the electrical workers would use stray cats — urged on by blasts of compressed air — to pull strings through long, narrow conduit pipes inside the dam. Once the howling, spitting animal came out the other side, the string would be used to pull a cord through the conduit, and then the cord used to pull heavy electrical cables into place. That was classic Depression-era workstyle; callous and innovative at the same time.

Heading southward from the dam, I followed the Grand Coulee, an old southern route the Columbia used after an invading finger of the Canadian glacier once blocked its ancestral path. Now much of the Coulee is a placid and sterile water impoundment (I refuse to call these things "lakes") used to store water for the dam. Steamboat Rock, a huge, mystical, boat-shaped mesa, stands in the middle of Grand Coulee. Impervious to the flood and all other forms of physical erosion, it succumbed to an erosion of spirit when the Bureau of Reclamation created an "Aqua Park" for water skiers at its base.

My first destination was Dry Falls, a great, semicircular arena, 400 feet high and 3½ miles across. At the peak of the flooding, it was four times the scale of Niagara. Bretz said so much water went over the escarpment that it wasn't even a real falls; it was *a rapid.* I parked the van and tried to avoid a clutch of other tourists as they shuffled down the path along the edge of the escarpment, videotaping as they walked. I felt vaguely antiquated, carrying a large, dog-eared book and a sheaf of notes instead of a camcorder.

The great escarpment, and its basin underneath, were truly dead things. Raptors of some kind circled silently in the updrafts along the ledge, and the whole post-catastrophic landscape was bathed in eerie quiet. There was no real channel upstream from the escarpment, just a broad, scoured basin. The reddish-brown basalt rock of the ledge itself was worn and fissured. Here and there yellowish tufts of bunch-grass clung to the face of the ancient spillway. Not a drop of water was going over the falls now, and only a few tiny sloughs dotted the huge outwash basin below. I felt like a visitor to some vast, alien graveyard.

The early Columbia River had begun the excavation of Dry Falls while it was diverted down Grand Coulee by glaciers, but the flood itself did most of the work. At full bore, the turbulence at the base of the falls was enough to rip out pickup-sized chunks of basalt and send them whirling to distant resting places downstream. (Some wound up as huge "haystack rocks" on distant fields, which were otherwise pure wind-driven loess.) The falls had actually begun its existence somewhere downstream, but the location moved rapidly upstream as the flood eroded the land away. In typical geological language — ponderous but with a hint of poetry — this great dead thing was called a "recessional cataract."

The small museum at the edge of the falls provided a large painting, an "artist's conception" (apparently this was meant as a scientific disclaimer) of what the flood looked like as it went over the falls. The painting had everything — the crashing regional, map-sheet-wide flood, the boulders being plucked from the face of the escarpment, the intruding Okanagan lobe of the Cordilleran glacier looming in the background, and massive icebergs calving off. I recalled the childhood envy I harbored for these painters of museum dioramas and illustrators of dinosaur books. We sanction these people to visualize; we give them rights to create a reality for us. Harlen Bretz had no such sanction, and was a skeptical scientist as well, but he visualized anyway, and on a grand scale. Wearing his usual khaki shirt with sleeves rolled up, wire-frame glasses, and custom White boots from Spokane, he did not look the part of a visionary. All his career he was an advocate of field work, of deduction based on field observation. Yet this hard-nosed, tin-hatted redneck produced a phenomenal, unprecedented landscape vision.

I left Dry Falls and the Grand Coulee, heading westward to rejoin the Columbia in its present-day course, and to spend the night in Wenatchee. The next morning I got up early, eager to maintain the focus of the previous day. Over breakfast and coffee I read the skimpy details of Bretz's personal life: born in Michigan in 1882, attended college there and then became a teacher in Seattle. I realized with a mild shock that he had taught at the same high school that I went to, and then I reflected that the coincidence was quite logical, that some personal volatile could seep into the walls of that ancient school building, and precipitate decades later into the substrate of a heedless and distracted student.

Bretz took an active interest in the Pleistocene geology of the Puget Sound area, and his PhD thesis for the University of Chicago became the first comprehensive explanation of the impact of glaciation on the Puget Sound Lowlands. Upon graduation he was hired by the University of Washington, but this very practical, field-oriented geologist clashed with the abstract dons of UW's Geology Department, and he soon returned to the University of Chicago. It was there, in the course of teaching field geology courses, that Bretz was first introduced to the shattered landscapes of eastern Washington, and a lifelong bond was created.

Driving southward out of Wenatchee, I followed the valley of the Columbia, passing through suburbs, then orchards, and finally back to basalt bedrock, and the rhythm of the trip was quickly re-established. The Columbia had cut deeply into the ancient basalt lava beds, which towered above me. The beds were layered, not from volcanic eruptions, but from repeated flows that broke through the earth's crust and spread out over level ground. Some of the basalt layers were outrageous, geometrically perfect eight-sided columns; others were pillowy, twisted, upswept and bronzed. Artists and sculptors would simply have to stand aside to these materials, techniques, and finish. If there were an art of basalt, it would be properly called Monumental. Here were not only locked files on the life of central Washington in the Miocene, but some of the keys to landscape itself. The members and entablatures of these basalt beds were ultimately a sculpted and bronzed language, absolutely free of human concern.

I eventually found a back road — just a faint line on my map — that allowed me to leave the Columbia again and head eastward, back into the heart of the scablands. Palisades Road it was called, and after ten minutes of driving I realized it was taking me up one of the outflows of Moses Coulee, the westernmost of the flood's recessional cataracts. I reminded myself, as Bretz no doubt did over and over, to anyone who would listen, that these great gouges were not old river *valleys,* they were old river *beds.* Looking at a satellite photograph of east-central Washington is like looking down on a newly seeded lawn that was watered too heavily. It is a mass of braided channels and gullies that separate, rejoin, and then separate again.

The same ramparts of layered basalt I had seen along the Columbia followed me along the Palisades Road, and the scree slopes of broken basalt along the rampart bases had all reached an identical angle of repose. Butte and basin is what geologists call this landscape, and I am satisfied with that name.

The great Irish-Canadian artist Paul Kane sketched the basalt landscapes of the Columbia in 1847. In his journals, he talks of being careful not to dramatize the sketches in any way, for fear that he would be accused of fabricating fantastic landscapes to sell to a gullible European audience, eager for images of the wild Western Interior.

I stopped to stretch my legs a bit. Walking towards the base of the scree, I passed through a clump of shoulder-height big sagebrush plants. The odor they released was powerful and evocative after such a long absence; that was the odor of a whole bioregion, the perfume of the Columbia Basin. If I were ever to feel the need for a scent for my body, an olfactory signature, it would be that of sagebrush, no question.

After another hour of slowly driving through the deserted

coulee, it struck me that I had not passed a single car. I had the scablands to myself, just as Harlen Bretz did in 1923. He would have been the young graduate student from the University of Chicago, roaming the sparsely-settled basin in hardhat and battered vehicle, summer after summer, marshalling his own urgencies, fending off bachelor farmers driven mad by isolation and drought, visualizing aerial photographs when none existed, and slowly collecting fragments for what was to become his vast regional mosaic. My problem with Bretz and his work is this: do I approach the man's life through simple exposition, or do I try to give voice to the quixotic absorption and mystery that must have been such a large part of his life? Anyone who can say:

> ideas without precedent are generally looked on with disfavor and men are shocked if their conceptions of an orderly world are challenged. A hypothesis earnestly defended begets emotional reaction which may cloud the protagonists view, but if such hypotheses outrage prevailing modes of thought, the view of antagonists may also become fogged

was not an ordinary man, subject to the usual set of motives.

Long before the flood, the stage of the Columbia Basin was set first by a meteor impact, then a lava flow, then a regional tilting, then a millennial dust storm and finally, the glacier. The meteor is thought to have struck somewhere in northeastern Oregon, permanently fracturing the earth's crust, and releasing the multiple outpourings of lava that flowed northward to fill the basin and create the layers of basalt. Tectonic forces then picked up the whole basin and tilted it, so Spokane was on the high end and Pasco, near the present Oregon border, was on the low end. Thousands of years of dust storms followed, and the basalt was gradually covered with a thick layer of fine silt (loess). Then the glaciers had their day. Glaciers are curious animals, which can grow and retreat at the same time. The Purcell lobe, a narrow, active finger of the Cordilleran glacier, muscled its way down the Kootenay valley, across the present-day British Columbia border and into northern Idaho, to butt up against the last rampart of the Bitterroot Range. This glacial finger formed a giant plug, stopping all the natural westward drainage out of the mountains of Idaho and Montana. At the same time, the main body of the huge Cordilleran glacier was melting, releasing vast quantities of water, and the result was Glacial Lake Missoula. (One can stand in present-day Missoula and look up to the lake's high water mark on the hillside, 900 feet above town.) The mechanism was now set for Bretz's flood. Continued filling of the lake weakened the plug of ice. Buoyancy may have lifted it, water pressure may have cracked it, warming waters may have undermined it; no one knows for sure. But one fine day, about 12,500 years ago, the plug gave way, and 700 *cubic miles* of water roared out through the narrow mountain gap, moving at a speed of fifty miles an hour. Once the flood passed over Spokane, it split into a northern channel that followed the Columbia/Grand Coulee/Dry Falls route, a central channel that passed over Crab Creek and Odessa, and a southern channel that went south-ward towards the Tri-Cities and the Snake River. The Palouse, that great fertile mound of loess in southeastern Washington, was left untouched. The glacial lake emptied in the space of three or four days, and all was quiet again. Then the glacial plug reformed, Lake Missoula began to fill again, and some 50 years later, it flushed itself across the scablands a second time. This happened about three dozen times before the glacial epoch finally lost its grip.

"No vestige of a beginning, no prospect of an end." That is how the pioneer geologist James Hutton (1726-1797) described a revolutionary new view of the earth's development, which grew into the geological doctrine known as Uniformitarianism. Known processes of erosion, volcanism, faulting and uplift, operating over long periods of time, could explain all the earth's landforms, Hutton said. In the early 1900s, the growing weight of evidence against Creationism as a popular explanation of earth history finally caused it to collapse. William Jennings Bryan fought Creationism's last good fight at the Scopes "Monkey Trials" in 1925. Uniformitarian earth scientists and evolutionary biologists finally gained the right to ply their trade in the full light of day. Then in the midst of this great paradigm shift, a respected, bright young geologist, one of science's own, published an account of an apocalyptic, doom-cracking, mega-biblical and continental-scale flood. His first comprehensive paper was published in 1925, the same year of Bryan's defeat. A Scientist/Catastrophist had gone public, and it was heresy. His fellow scientists closed ranks; he was not believed.

Early in his career, Bretz convinced himself that the entire Channelled Scabland was a post-flood landscape, but he did not make an initial connection with Glacial Lake Missoula. So he was plagued with the problem of finding a large enough body of water to generate his flood (the only missing element, he lamented during this time, was "the hydraulics of the concept"). In 1927, the Geological Society of Washington, D.C., convened a special meeting to debate the flood hypothesis. The meeting was a set-up; Bretz was the lone proponent of the flood and the rest of the agenda was stacked with the doubting heavyweights of geological science: Alden, Gilluly, Meinzer, and McKnight. One of their main points of attack was the water source issue. Bretz was savaged. Sitting quietly in the audience at that Washington meeting was another geologist by the name of J.T. Pardee, who was an authority on Glacial Lake Missoula. As Bretz was being grilled, Pardee reportedly leaned over to a colleague and whispered, "I know where Bretz's flood came from," but he had no intention of publicly identifying himself with this young Turk. So Bretz soldiered on alone, eventually making the glacial lake connection himself, and developing the complete Glacial Lake Missoula/Spokane Flood/Channelled Scabland theory in place by 1930, one of the most daring hypotheses in the annals of contemporary science. In my own more obscure annals, he will be known for the re-imagining of a landscape that was totally lost to human memory.

There is a photograph of Bretz, taken when he was 94. He is in his booklined study, and has a big coffee mug in one hand and is gesturing with the other hand, making a point. He must have been outside shortly before the photograph was taken, since he is still wearing a windbreaker. In spite of his large frame, he looks a bit like Gandhi, with bald head, wire-frame glasses and remarkable eyes. He has the look of a man who had spiritual experiences, albeit scientific ones, a man who wore his obsessions well, a man who could deal with thirty years of professional rejection.

The Palisades Road came out at Soap Lake. From there, I took a long detour southward to see the Wallula Gap, south of Pasco. This is where the Columbia cuts through the Horse Heaven Hills, a low range that runs parallel to the Washington-Oregon border. The gap was a narrow choke-point for the floodwaters, which forced all the separate braided channels back together. Another vast but temporary lake was created along the base of the hills as a result. Just north of the Gap, I passed the confluence of the Snake and the Columbia rivers. If we were to grant these rivers any spiritual significance, here would certainly be the place to celebrate it. Their combined drainage extends into magnificent landscapes in five U.S. states and one Canadian province. The rock I skip on the Kootenay River that runs through my home town of Nelson is lifted by water that runs down through the gap.

I gritted my teeth as I drove past the confluence. There was no park, no oasis for spirit. The union of two of the greatest rivers of the continent was celebrated with a tank farm, a trailer court, and a pulp mill.

The highway through the gap was squeezed between the basalt cliffs and the water. I got off the highway on a tiny pullout and clambered over guardrail, woven-wire fence and railway tracks to get down to water level. Winds out of the basin poured through the gap and whitecaps danced over the water. I took a dubious picture of the two opposing ramparts, only as insurance against some distant day when I might forget.

Harlen Bretz lived to see his work and his theory vindicated, thanks primarily to his longevity (he died in 1971, still lucid at ninety-eight years old). Curiously, when the Viking orbiter began transmitting the first close-up photographs of Mars in 1976, Bretz's work was found to be a great asset in helping to explain the ancient flood structures on that planet's ravaged surface. Harlen Bretz's theory of the Great Spokane Flood,[1] and the subsequent reaction to the theory, is now a benchmark in the study of science.

The dilemma of how best to present this material remains. A colleague of mine offered one surprisingly logical solution;

he knew I was preoccupied with the Bretz/scablands story and once inquired, "well, how's the Bretz play coming along?" Perhaps it is time we begin addressing geology in theatre.

I headed north again, to the ripple marks of Odessa, and then on to Spokane. I was content. I had seen the giant ripples, and floated with the hawks over the bones of Dry Falls. Too often I am satisfied with the superficial appreciation of material that fascinates me, but this time I had taken Bretz and his scablands to a deeper level. Understanding the geography of a place, the relations of its rivers and the forces of its geology, is a kind of transformative act. At a certain point, literal information can change to spirit and essence. Our well-being has always depended on the mystery and complexity of the wilderness, and exploration of new places is almost a genetic trait. Now that new lands are completely gone and wilderness is nearly gone, we must turn the telescope of exploration around, to find mystery and complexity in the fine details of what is left.

Approaching Spokane from the west, I saw a huge B-52 bomber circling above it, like some obscene icon. I realized the route I had chosen would take me past Fairchild Air Force Base, home of the B-52 squadron and the focus of some old anger. I had not seen Fairchild for twenty-five years, so I slowed down to have a look. The strip of tacky low-rise motels was the same, but the base itself seemed less imposing than it did in 1971, when I delivered myself there for a Draft induction physical and a truly memorable discussion about the nature of conscientious objection to war. The experience also confirmed what was then just a tentative personality trait — the unwillingness to belong to organizations. Fairchild had demythologized itself over the intervening twenty-five years; it looked a bit neglected and only a single MP guarded the front gate. The parade ground had been converted to an intriguing obstacle course, complete with ropes, climbing towers and water hazards, and I had read somewhere that the B-52s were being slowly cut up for scrap.

Eastern Washington had been my home for some years, but I left shortly after my first experience at Fairchild, no longer able to tolerate the smug attitudes, the intolerance for dissent, and the war in Vietnam. In returning on this visit, I found that the basin landscape still retained its mythic qualities and the politics, fortunately, had changed. Now I had Bretz, plus the ongoing private joy of these remembered landscapes, from the distant days of pheasant hunting in outwash coulees and hitchhiking the backroads, free from the veneer of anger. My departure from the basin was probably inevitable; our chords would never have fit. But now the temporary spasm of Fairchild and Vietnam has been replaced by the enduring warp and complexity of this flood-scarred land itself, and I enjoyed a modest sense of repossession.

1. The name diminishes the event, which actually spanned a thousand-mile axis from Deer Lodge, Montana, to Astoria, Oregon.

4

Fossicking on the Border

It was inevitable that a re-exploration would draw me to the ambiguities of the border. Politics, once laid crudely and arbitrarily across a latitude, split a single region into two different identities. Then in the subtle, ongoing confusion of culture and landscape, those differences ultimately become real.

Peter, my friend from Vancouver, came with me on the first border foray. He was studying the journals of members of the original U.S./Canadian Boundary Survey party, and we had met through a mutual friend. He and I were close enough in age to be contemporaries, and I was willing to violate my rule of solitary re-exploration because I sensed a kindred spirit.

We started out on the Salmo River, on the Canadian side. The Salmo starts near Nelson and flows southward uninterrupted almost to the border, where it joins the much larger Pend Oreille River[1] on its northward loop into Canada. We agreed that the Salmo had no real connection with the border, but it was on the way and we thought it might be good fishing water. Besides, there was a roadless stretch of the Salmo called Shenango Canyon that I wanted to reconnoiter. Locales with place names like Shenango call out to me, and we were not pressed for time.

The Salmo did turn out to be good water. It had a bottom

of rounded, watermelon-sized rocks with bigger boulders here and there, boulders that harbored interesting backeddies and riffles and logjams. This was September, and if you picked a wide spot and took your time, you could wade from one side of the river to the other, following whims and possibilities. Peter and I did that, splitting up in a gentlemanly, fly-fishing sort of way, each vying for the poorest-looking spot to start fishing in. After ten minutes I realized we were in world-class water indeed, doctor/lawyer water. In fact, I found a shiny surgeon's hemostat lying on the bottom, confirming the presence of doctors. Ordinary mortals like Peter and I would not remove hooks with tools of surgical steel.

I fished my way downstream and got close enough to the mouth of Shenango Canyon to have a look. It was not a major canyon, but there was a visible break in the angle of the water surface as it ratcheted downward at the entrance. The boulders in the water got bigger, and the hillsides swept up more steeply, with bare rock outcrops visible. Shenango's forest was a cornucopia of species: looking only casually, I saw cedar, Douglas-fir, hemlock, aspen, cottonwood, ponderosa, lodge-pole and white pine, plus larch and yew. I marked it as a place to come back to.

The fish were not biting, so we drove on down to Nelway, a tiny village at the border crossing. Peter wanted to walk a stretch of the actual border, but neither of us had any idea how the authorities — or even remote sensing devices — might react to two middle-aged men on foot, with backpacks. We decided to follow the Pend Oreille for a while and then try to reach the border at a more isolated spot. As we drove, we compared notes on isolated border crossings we knew: Nighthawk, Yahk, Rykerts, Chopaka and so on. Peter knew far more of these places than I did.

The Pend Oreille River is shackled by three dams along this stretch: Boundary Dam just as it crosses from Washington into British Columbia, the Sevenmile Dam, midway along the Canadian loop, and the Waneta Dam as the river joins the Columbia on its way back into Washington. We detoured onto a steep trail that took us right down to the reservoir created by Sevenmile, and then scrambled on foot back upstream along steep, lifeless shore and slack water. On undammed rivers, water levels vary predictably by season and by year, a kind of variation plant life understands and copes with. Water levels on dammed rivers vary unpredictably within seasons based on electrical need, so all of these shackled rivers — the Columbia, the Kootenay, the Pend Oreille — have lifeless bands of foreshore that are beyond the powers of plants to colonize. Scrambling further, we could just make out Boundary Dam in the distance. Boundary is owned outright by the power utility of the City of Seattle, and much of the power from the two Canadian dams is sold to large urban areas in the U.S. I speculated aloud to Peter how satisfying it might be to bring some of the good people of Seattle out here, one at a time, so they could know the actual price the river pays for them to run their Cuisinarts and cappuccino machines.

The clear, sluggish water in dam reservoirs does favor fish raptors, such as ospreys and eagles, and we did catch a glimpse of an eagle overhead. It had a branch in its mouth about the length and thickness of a broom handle.

Getting back on the single-track logging road that clung to the mountainside above the river, I was reminded how steep the Kootenay (and Kutenai, on the American side) country really is. I was glad of Peter's four-wheel drive, and found myself hugging my elbows to my sides, an unconscious effort to ease our passage along the narrow road. The CB radio chatter in these mountains is full of cryptic announcements like "Gold Creek, 13, unloaded," or "Teepee, 25, loaded," which gives log truck drivers a very necessary and very precise sense of just when and where they will meet oncoming trucks.

Part of my adjustment to the landscape of the mountains has meant coming to terms with this steepness, and what it meant for my sense of distance, my psyche, and my sense of belonging. Steepness has to be assimilated here, in all its manifestations: the abbreviation of sunrises and sunsets; the buildup of calf muscles; the overcoming of acrophobia. The potent duality of mountain and valley must also be assimilated. Life is mostly carried on between 400 and 800 metres in the bottoms of these steep, confused valleys, but the landscape only becomes clear and obvious from the tops of the ridges, at 1,500 metres and upward. Valley orientation, whether north-south or east-west, becomes biologically important: the east-west valleys capture more sunlight, but north-south valleys are corridors for the movement of weather, species and large rivers. The valley orientations often bear no relation to the older bearings of the mountains. Just when I think I have a grasp of the lay of a particular Kootenay landscape, an anomalous valley or ridgeline cuts transversely through my understanding.

Continuing westward along the Pend Oreille toward the Columbia, we came upon an abandoned orchard, and Peter, an avid birder, stopped the car and pulled out his field glasses virtually in a single motion. He was pleased to describe for me a bright, canary-like western tanager, which I finally located with the glasses. A little way further on, he pointed out a brilliant blue lazuli bunting.

A friend who lived in this valley as a child, before the dams, the relocations, and the flooding, told me the Pend Oreille valley was once known for its curative properties. Hot summer sun would heat up the pines and firs high up on the rocky, south-facing slopes, and in the evening, cool air would flood down those same slopes, carrying the forest's aromatic essences down into the valley below, where they acted as a balm to congested lungs and spirits. As a contemporary visitor, I could certainly visualize the original valley as restorative, whether I believed in the medical value of forest aromatics or not.

The advancing day drew us forward, into itself. I was able to try out some very frivolous and scandalous ideas on Peter, ideas that had been bottled up for some time, and needed to see the light of day. We took a short side hike to see a waterfall, and spent some time speculating on fates in a tiny graveyard. I proposed a term for our activities: fossicking, a kind of relaxed, omnivorous exploration that embraces all tangible and intangible aspects of the landscape. To fossick was originally an Australian word for random, overland gold prospecting, an activity sufficiently distant and obscure that I felt confident about modifying the term for my own ends. Like any number of other outdoor pursuits — and fly-fishing is a prime example — our fossicking provided a purposeful guise for the simple enjoyment of nature. This trip had had absolutely no prospect of economic gain attached. It was a brief escape into the noneconomic, lyrical, perhaps even nonrational dimension, that some of us never do, and none of us can do for very long. It was, in a word, frivolous, but I freely acknowledge a personal tendency to be very serious about frivolity.

While we stopped for lunch, I leafed through the elegantly bound 1866 journals of the Englishman John Keast Lord, which Peter had brought along. Lord was a member of the U.S./Canadian Boundary Survey, and his claustrophobic impression of this part of the Kootenays is evident in this passage:

> ...impassable barriers of mountains, so closely piled and wooded that the valleys between them were little else than rocky gorges, devoid of grass or other food for pack animals.

He is much kinder to the Colville valley, in northeastern Washington:

> ...The Colville valley is, roughly speaking, about thirty miles long, the hills on one side being densely studded with pine trees, and the other quite clear of timber, but thickly clothed up to their rounded summits with the bunchgrass.

Lord was here referring to a key geographical dynamic of the valleys of the Kootenays: the relative dryness of the east sides of north-south valleys, like the Colville, and of the north sides of east-west-trending valleys, like the one in which Nelson resides.

Lord was a veterinarian by trade, and showed an earnest, methodical interest in mammals, insects and aquatic life in his journals. He described both the tanager and the bunting, confirming the two species as long-term residents of the Kootenays. He also described the delightful little horned toad as occurring on the Canadian side of the valleys of the Columbia, Kootenay and Flathead rivers.

One of the benefits of middle age is the ability to support several obsessions at once and, because reptiles are one of mine, I knew that there have been no confirmed sightings of the horned toad in southern British Columbia in contemporary times. Some curious phenomenon, some unknown natural or human-caused event, has extirpated them since Lord's time. I filed that bit of information away for further investigation. Reptiles, which loomed so large in our ancient mythologies, have become incidental curiosities in modern life. The obscure ecology of the horned toad at the northern edge of its range could actually turn out to be a powerful, even symbolic illustration of the dynamics of nature itself. We have found great social and personal analogies in the laws of physics over the last few decades — words like entropy, fusion, meltdown and so on have become household terms. Perhaps we are now entering an age where the laws of biology, ecology, and the horned toad will take on social relevance.

I closed Lord's book carefully and put it back in Peter's knapsack. A third language, a third discipline, would have to be added to my re-exploration work, along with science and spirituality: lore. Lore — the oral and written observations of nature and the human experience of the region, both contemporary and historical — has its own language and its own discipline, and helps make a region what it is. Nature does not invest certain landscapes with a sense of romance, or foreboding, or freedom: we do that. We can actually quantify the value we vest in a landscape from which a large body of water can be seen: realtors tell me that an ocean or lake view will add 20 per cent to the value of a lot. The totally artificial observations, distinctions and stories we humans invest in nature become, paradoxically, important.

Still in search of an isolated stretch of border, we crossed the Pend Oreille at the Sevenmile Dam, on to the narrow sliver of land between the river's Canadian loop and the 49th parallel. Prospects looked good as we headed southward on an isolated logging road, switchbacking along hillsides clothed in second-growth cedar. Finally we glimpsed the razor-sharp cutline through the trees on a distant mountainside.

We continued on the logging road as far south as we could, and then struck out on foot, stumbling through the dense cedar on a thirty-degree slope. The border in this forested part of the world has its own manner of optical illusion. The cutline is of course always glimpsed on the hillside opposite to the one you are on, and it is nearly impossible to project the exact location of that cutline on to your side of the valley. Based on our glimpse of the border on the far hillside, we could be anywhere from five minutes to an hour away from it. Fortunately, after fifteen minutes of side-hill scrambling, a bright green strip appeared ahead, contrasting strongly with the muted greys and browns of the cedars around us. Immediately I started looking for laser beams and trip wires. A rancher friend who lives near an isolated part of the border told me he once crossed it briefly on horseback to retrieve an errant bull. Having coffee in town the next day, one of the local RCMP asked the rancher how he had made out with that Angus bull. Border country is full of these kinds of stories.

Finally we emerged into the sunlight and Douglas maple of the ten-metre-wide strip, and chose adjoining stumps to sit on. I was nervous, but Peter was happy. He described how the survey party would have dealt with this drainage; one crew would work its way laboriously to the new ridge, while another crew stayed on this one, still in sight of the last surveyed ridge behind them. When the lead crew reached the top of the new ridge, they would set up their instruments. In these dense forests, younger party members probably climbed trees to provide the first sightlines. They would establish a bearing, and then work back and forth until 49 degrees, 0 minutes and 0 seconds was found. Then the whole operation would advance by one ridge.

The survey party used Fort Colville, near the present-day Washington community of Kettle Falls, as a wintering camp and provisioning point. The fort was located near a traditional aboriginal fishing area, a series of rapids on the Columbia that were well known by everyone in the Interior as a place to meet, rest, gather information and food. Today the Fort and the rapids are underwater, a victim of the Grand Coulee dam.

The border was not always the visceral reality on the landscape that it is now. Wallace Stegner, in his book *Wolf Willow*, described life in an isolated town on the Saskatchewan-Montana border in the early part of the century. People moved unhindered across the border, and few of them knew, or cared, exactly where it was. That all changed, Stegner says, when Canada sent troops to Europe at the beginning of World War I, and the United States stayed neutral. The border became even more precisely defined in the 1920s when the U.S. went dry, Canada stayed wet, and crossborder bootlegging became a growth industry.

Borders always have a kind of uncertainty and tension, and I find the same qualities in my relationship to them. The tension multiplied as I crossed and recrossed the border during the Vietnam War. Borders are geographically precise, but mentally ambiguous. When I was young I dreamed of unknown and faraway places in Canada: now I dream occasionally of remembered landscapes in the U.S. As a student of border differences in accent, language and outlook, I frequently get lost in the phenomenon of observer proximity. Like the physicist and the elusive atom, the act of observation changes the observed.

My first few weeks actually resident in Canada were spent in Edmonton, Alberta, in the wintertime. I was daunted by the bitter cold and the darkness, and promptly moved further south. To this day I still have ambivalent feelings about those vast northern stretches across the tops of the provinces and into the Territories; they may be the next frontier for me. Landscapes that inspire fear also attract.

There is a curious development inversion that takes place around the border in this part of the world. Often the Canadian side is populated and developed, while the adjacent American side is hinterland. That is part of the weird alchemy of borders: the least desirable land and climate on one side of a border may be the most sought after on the other.

Peter and I finally left our stumps on the border strip, rejoined the logging road, and followed the Pend Oreille out to its junction with the Columbia. This great regional confluence was celebrated with another dam, the Waneta. When we hit pavement, we knew our border fossick was over, and started reluctantly for home.

A week later I went back to Shenango Canyon alone, to let go the last shards of inhibition between myself and the landscape, to drop the borders. Shenango. I rolled it on my tongue, over and over. If I lived in, came from, this Shenango, would I be different? Would the watermelon rocks have influenced me? Do we dwellers of the Ktunaxa[2], which we separately corrupt as either Kutenai or Kootenay, have more in common with each other than with our urban compatriots in Seattle or Vancouver? The sense of place is truly an elective affinity: you can choose to let it influence you, or you can choose not to. It comes down to a question of borders.

I had my pole with me on the second trip as well, mainly to provide some rational excuse for wading hip-deep down a river. Occasionally I would take a cast, but mainly I let the fly just drift ahead of me. I wore old tennis shoes whose soles were worn thin, so my feet could sense the surfaces and textures of the slippery watermelon rocks. I worked my way down beyond the point I had reached last time, to where I felt the river channel narrow. In the still pools, the clear water magnified the river bed. I wanted suddenly, passionately, to learn every inch of the river's Shenango reach.

Most of nature is no longer wilderness, but this was, albeit a very small piece. The theoreticians tell me that wilderness as a place is shortly to become extinct, and that rather than devoting my energies to preserving the last remaining shreds of it, I must find and appreciate the individual qualities that make up wilderness in the rest of nature, even if it is an irrigation ditch or a vacant lot. Wildness, they call it, the individual mechanisms and species and essences that together make a wilderness. God, as they say, is found in the details. We residents of the Western Interior possess a kind of arrogance based on lifetimes of inhabiting huge tracts of natural and seminatural space, and often find urban preoccupations with a single tree or tiny plot of ground downright silly. But just as arrogance and humility can both be valuable human emotions, so are wilderness and wildness, I tell myself. I see the validity of what the theoreticians are saying but, from the perspective of hip-deep in the Salmo as it passes through Shenango Canyon, it will be tough. I will honestly try to drop my fondness for wilderness and come to love wildness, too, but I must be let down easy.

A large whaleback of dense, grainy basement rock broke

the water surface ahead of me, and I moved closer to marvel at it. Its surface was full of unexpected curves, channels and cuppings. Like a Henry Moore sculpture, the black rock stood muscular and sexual, with an ambiguity about whether its origin was worked or natural. River water sluiced over parts of the whaleback, and was held still in others. I searched the nearby shore until I found a round, marble-sized rock, and put it gently into the bottom of one of the circular depressions that had water running over it. Sure enough, the small rock began to rotate slowly in the force of the current. This whaleback could easily grace a public square in a large city, I thought. Adults could see it as an evocative sculpture and graceful fountain, while children could appreciate the small geological nonsense machine contained in it.

Before I went any further, I put my wallet and fishing license inside a plastic bag I had brought for fish, and tied it snugly. Everything else could get wet, I decided. I was going to make a day of it. Norman MacLean was right: in the end all things become one, and a river runs through it. The water moved around my legs with authority now, questioning any movement that was not directly downstream. I advanced slowly, forward foot sliding, toe pointed, following the surface of each rounded rock down to tricky, unknown footholds at the bottom. It was a kind of fly-fisher's ballet, taking small leaps of faith and striving for grace in the separate medium of the waters of Shenango.

---

1. Locally pronounced as "Ponderay."
2. Roughly, ke-tu-na-ha.

5

Cowboy Fiction

THE LANDSCAPES OF THE NORTH AMERICAN WEST, with their enduring myths of frontier, new beginnings, and freedom, are pervaded by fiction. The American cowboy writer and painter Will James lived that fiction. He came west, assembled a complete new personal mythology, and in the end, saw his mythology become a fate. Most of us allow fiction to penetrate only as far as our bookshelves, stopping it far short of personal identity. Will James did not. He created himself as the main character in his own novels: cowboy, painter, writer, western myth and finally, victim.

I first became aware of James when I was a boy, reading his novel *Smoky, the Cow Horse*. The book was a handsome 1929 Scribner's edition, belonging to my father. He had read it as a boy too, when it was first published. *Smoky* was, and perhaps still is, the quintessential old-fashioned boy's illustrated adventure, in the tradition of G.A. Henty and Robert Louis Stevenson. The story features a lone rebellious figure, bonded to a half-wild horse, working with animals and against the elements, dealing rarely with other men and almost never with women. The prose of *Smoky*, as with all the James books, is written in a western vernacular. The illustrations were strongly influenced by James's contemporary Charles M. Russell, and the best of them rival that artist's work.

James portrayed himself as the quintessential American cowboy, but — thirty years after the first reading of *Smoky* — I stumbled across a reference to his clandestine beginnings in Canada. I was drawn to James again, but the real hook this time was not the dated and juvenile romance of his writing, but the sense that I might learn something from the man's overwhelming obsession with a certain kind of landscape, an obsession that caused him to bury one identity and create another.

Will James began life in 1892 as Ernest Nephtali Dufault, in St-Nazaire, Quebec. Family accounts say young Dufault spent all his spare time sketching horses and devouring dime westerns. He was consumed by the desire to be a cowboy, and at age fifteen he bolted, taking the train west to the Canadian prairies. For the next four years (1907-1911) he moved around the ranchlands of southern Alberta and southern Saskatchewan, and actually filed a homestead claim near the tiny Saskatchewan community of Val Marie, before his final bolt to the United States.

I decided to pay a visit to Val Marie, to sniff out what it was about its landscape that was so compelling to the young Will James, what it was that made him decide this particular West was real enough to file a claim on it. If I could understand some of this man's motives, they might shed some light on my own — and perhaps my father's — motives. I met Lise Perrault there; a lady rancher and landscape painter herself, she is a storehouse of information on Will James. She gave me directions to the homestead, just outside the newly-created Grasslands National Park. I followed a gravel road as it wound along beside the Frenchman River, in the center of a broad, dry valley. The dwarf river in its huge valley reminded me of Harlen Bretz. No doubt he could have re-animated the great Pleistocene events that had shaped the Frenchman.

When I got to the homestead quarter I climbed the valley side to a high vantage point. The road was visible, as was a small farmhouse, a quarter of recently broken land, and three aspen trees. All the rest, from horizon to horizon, was straw-yellow prairie, mottled here and there with darker patches of buckbrush. I realized I was looking at elements of *Line Camp*, one of James's more famous paintings, done in 1932, and generally considered to be inspired by the landscapes of the American Southwest. The foreground of that painting contains a low log cabin with a sod roof. A saddled horse stands near the cabin, a loose rope running from its bridle in through the open door. Smoke is coming from the cabin's stovepipe. The unseen cowboy would be inside making breakfast, while the horse awaits his companionship in the day's work. The short yellow grass in the foreground of the painting, the thick stand of brush in a distant coulee and the eroded, bluish headland on the horizon all spoke strongly of the very place where I sat.

I believe the four years in the Canadian prairies were seminal to James. Here would have been where he saw the first real images of the West and cattle ranching. The short-grass, dry coulees and badlands of Saskatchewan and Alberta became his first templates, into which he carved and fitted his own already powerful childhood vision of the West. Here is where he learned the technology of horse and cow and range, and where he changed from a gawky adolescent "not much good on a horse," into a skilled cowboy and horsebreaker.

In those same four prairie years he also shifted his language from French to western English. He dropped the francophone cadence of Ernest Nephtali Dufault in favor of the mono-syllabic "Will James." (These clipped and plosive Anglo-American names were somehow significant; all the characters of the James stories have names like "Clint," "Dan" and "Tom.") And he changed his identity, from Quebec immigrant to western cowboy.

Few people wrote things down in the southern Canadian prairies in the early 1900s; as a place in time it makes for poor history, but good fiction. Accounts of Dufault/James in those four years have him variously filing the homestead claim at Val Marie; working as a cowboy for the vast 76 Ranch near Swift Current; starting a little spread of his own near Ravenscrag, in the Cypress Hills country; and spending time in a Maple Creek jail. We also know he cowboyed in a line camp near Sage Creek, Alberta, from a surviving postcard.

Freedom of movement is central to the western myth, and

the creation of a multiple and simultaneous life is the ultimate freedom of movement. I saw this mechanism at work once before: many years ago I spent time travelling through small towns in southern New Mexico. Residents of nearly every community I visited volunteered the information that *theirs* was the town in which Pat Garrett had *actually* shot Billy the Kid. Will James created a similar, simultaneous multiple exposure; he mastered the reality of the Canadian prairies virtually as soon as he arrived, and so was free to explore other dimensions.

James found a mentor while in Saskatchewan, a fellow Québécois by the name of Pierre Beaupré, who helped James with the language transition and basic cowboy skills. Beaupré and James filed the Val Marie homestead claim jointly. Beaupré was a cultural intermediary, and significant enough to James that he wrote him into *The Lone Cowboy* (1930), his autobiographical fiction, as an adoptive father.

In *The Lone Cowboy*, James's mild Quebec parents are re-made into Texans who have bought a ranch in Montana. They are both killed while James is quite young, and "Bopy," a friend of the family, adopts and raises the child. Then Beaupré himself dies, drowning in an ice-filled Montana river. This piece of utter fiction leaves James totally free of the encumbrances of birth and family heritage, as well as explaining away his lifelong francophone accent.

Lise Perrault told me that Pierre Beaupré did exist and did not drown in Montana, but no one knows his real fate.

James then cuts off his actual family — father, mother and five Dufault siblings — in favor of the Montana fiction. After once departing Quebec, James returned there only twice in his life. The first trip was made about a year after he left, probably a social visit to show off the new chaps and the new mystique. The purpose of the second trip, made when James was beginning to gain national recognition for his writing and painting, was to burn all the letters he had written to his family, and to swear them to secrecy about his real identity.

James wrote and published a dozen books between 1926 and 1942, all of them about horses and cowboys, and all about himself, or rather the self he had created. Place names are virtually nonexistent in his texts, as are any verifiable historical events or figures. His "autobiography" is no exception. This man craved fame for the James persona and total anonymity for the Dufault.

The landscapes of the Interior often act as blank canvases into which we paint, and define, ourselves. Will James was a master at this: he created anonymous tableaux of corral, sagebrush and bucking horse, and inserted himself into them. His obsession with an anachronistic, dime-novel West, his secret identity, and a lifelong fear of the law (he spent two stints in jail) propelled this unlikely man into the realms of fiction and art. The cowboys of his drawings all look the same: long-waisted men with bowed legs and spurred boots, clad in white shirts and black vests, showing aquiline, hawk-nosed faces in profile. All of them have the handsome features of Ernest Dufault, idealized into a person he called Will James.

This is dangerous material. When we politely ask a new acquaintance where they are from, we are speaking from the instinctive belief that personal identity is partly created by place, that we will better understand that person by knowing the geographies of their past. What James did is take a conversational chestnut and raise it to the level of fierceness and obsession.

I looked across the Frenchman again. James chose to homestead in the only valley in Canada that contains both prairie dogs and horned toads, a valley that echoes the fauna of his future homes farther south.

James does refer to Canada in his works (*The Lone Cowboy, Winter Months in a Cow Camp*) but the reality is of course reversed: he writes himself coming into Canada as a young man on the run from U.S. law. He mentions no place names, but the "Cypress Ranch" of *Winter Months* is quite possibly the 76 Ranch, which James did work for and which, in those days, covered a good chunk of southern Saskatchewan.

James rode on into Montana, Nevada, Wyoming, Utah and Arizona and, eventually, to considerable fame as a writer/illustrator. His works provided American and Canadian readers — particularly eastern readers — with a clean, romantic vision of an era just past, and his persona let them believe that era still existed. It was predictable that Will James would eventually gravitate to Hollywood, first as a stunt rider and then as a collaborator on movie scripts about himself. He suffered the usual psychological dislocations of the American celebrity, made worse by his fear of discovery. He often binged on hard liquor. I think he was so good at everything that he drank as a self-imposed limitation. Will James wanted to show he could impair himself and *still* be good at everything.

By the late 1930s, his career in decline from drink and illness, James reached back to the Montana of his imagined ancestry, to the heart of the heart of the country, and bought a ranch in the Pryor Mountains south of Billings. Even that did not give him peace. His health continued to deteriorate and he died in 1942, of chronic liver failure.

The exile must project himself into a new culture. The rural exile must project himself into a new landscape as well. Saskatchewan and Alberta provided Will James with his first real western landscapes; these would imprint over the barns and orchard grass pastures of tamed and settled Quebec, already blurred by the strength of his youthful vision of the West. Yet the real landscapes of exile will never quite match the imagined ones, so the immigrant is condemned to an endless search for the perfect diorama. Good work for a painter.

The Frenchman River country southeast of Val Marie is certainly the High Lonesome, and one never arrives there by accident. Nature and space surround you in an unbroken expanse right to the horizon. The country could be the backdrop for the ultimate western movie — one that deals not with childish gun-fascination and cardboard good and evil, but with our place in nature, and nature's place in us. A western of the Interior.

I left the valley with some sense of completion, of closing the Will James chapter. James was not a particularly important writer, although he has probably claimed an enduring place within the faded and tattered genre of the western novel.[1] I value him primarily as a theorist — one who postulated a bizarre and romantic link between place and self, who embraced a landscape in the primal act of creating a unique personal culture. The energy of his stories and paintings came from the same source that Barry Lopez described — the difference between the inner landscape and the outer one. I realized that James's obsession was not with the land itself, but land with the human totally and perfectly rooted within it. Landscape with figures, so to speak.

I also value James on a personal and family level. At age fifteen my father also crossed the continent on a westbound train, alone. That was twenty-five years after James did, and the circumstances were different. Whether he took the copy of *Smoky* with him, and what particular combination of landscape and desire his head was full of, I am not given to know. But in considering my father's solitary train trip through the western space, I think I hear a faint echo of Will James.

Fiction inevitably becomes personal. A few books will move beyond the bookshelf and intrude on to the margins of a reader's life, as James's have on to the margins of mine. His books have linked father, author and son within a nested set of landscape dreams.

---

1. It is a testimony to the power of the cowboy mythology that the activities of riding, roping, branding and so on — which at most consume a few weeks of a *real* cowboy's year — are made into an entire lifestyle.

6

Cycles of Fire

TOMMY SHERMAN AND I WERE FRIENDS, and Tommy suffered for that. We were twelve, and lived on the same schoolbus route in a rural community called Dungeness. Tommy's father had a dairy farm down by the river, which he ran like a boot camp, with his five kids as recruits. Whenever I visited the Sherman farm, it seemed logical for Tommy and me to start up the old Massey tractor, or climb the steel silo to scratch our initials on the top, or other things that Tommy would never do on his own.

The event that ended my visits to the farm began inside a tree. Sherman's home pasture was a long, narrow one that lay between the river on one side and the county road on the other. At one time the land supported a dense forest of western red cedar, but some early Olympic Peninsula settler had logged it, stumped it, and put in a cow pasture. For some reason though, a single cedar, a massive old veteran, was left to mutter on into old age in the center of the pasture, amongst the thistle and orchard grass. One day Tommy and I had a footrace out to the tree. As we sprawled in the grass at the base of the tree, gasping for breath, I noticed a narrow opening in between the great muscular folds of the cedar's trunk. It looked just wide enough for us to squeeze through. Soon I had us both convinced that the hole inside the tree would have to contain the nest of an interesting wild animal, like a bat or maybe a raccoon. By turning sideways and inching forward headfirst, we were able to wriggle through the narrow cleft, one after the other, until we both stood up inside the cavernous center of the tree. One moment we were in sunny, everyday cow pasture and now we were in a narrow and ancient wooden tomb, whose stale air was rank with the smell of cedar. I fumbled for the matches it pleased me to carry around, and lit one. To our surprise, we saw that the inside walls of the tree were covered with long, fine, almost fur-like strips of wood. One by one, the darkness consumed all of my matches, and we saw no evidence of wild animals. After the last match went out, we noticed several glowing red points in the cedar fur in front of us. We slapped the points out as best we could, and crawled back out into the sunshine in search of other adventures.

Tommy didn't get on the schoolbus the next morning, but that wasn't unusual: his dad often kept him home to work. The first indication that anything was wrong came when the bus made an unscheduled stop alongside Sherman's river pasture. Several men and pieces of heavy equipment were gathered on the road, and I went to the front of the bus to have a look. Two men had chainsaws, and bright new sawdust was scattered all over. Great chunks of salmon-colored wood lay on the black asphalt. Both the power and phone lines were cut, and a lineman was putting on his spikes, getting ready to climb one of the poles. Fences were down on both sides of the road. Nobody on the bus knew what had happened. Through some blazing stroke of juvenile dissociation, I simply stared innocently, fascinated by the event, the men, and the fact that we were definitely going to be late for school.

As I continued to watch the scene in front of me, something, some nagging bit of incompleteness finally forced my attention away from the road over to Sherman's river pasture alongside. Slowly the realization dawned: there was something radically, horribly wrong with the pasture. The old cedar tree, which had stood there at least since we had moved to Dungeness and most probably since the beginning of time, was absolutely, irrevocably gone. All that remained was a blackened stump, plus the great long line of freshly cut chunks of wood that stretched from the stump, to the edge of Sherman's pasture, across the road and well over into Lotzgesell's pasture on the other side. I quietly returned to my seat and opened my geography schoolbook, in search of a distant unnamed island.

That incident is somehow symbolic of the triangular conundrum of trees, humans and fire. The single western red cedar in Sherman's pasture had no defences whatever to fire, and fell easy prey to my indiscriminate matches. Ponderosa pine, in contrast, not only survives fire, but actually thrives on it. Recently, I had the chance to watch a prescribed fire work its way harmlessly through a mixed stand of ponderosa pine in the Rocky Mountain Trench of southeastern British Columbia. The mature ponderosas had thick, flaky "puzzle bark" that simply refused to burn, although admittedly, no one was starting fires *inside* those trees.

We are slowly coming to the realization that the drier landscapes of North America — forests, grasslands, shrublands and even deserts — have evolved in the presence of periodic fires. We are also discovering that these ecosystems contain many species that are either fire-adapted, like the ponderosa, or fire-dependent, like the lodgepole pine. Fire-adapted species grow most successfully in the presence of fire; those that are fire-dependent ultimately cannot survive without it. Even some of the wetter forest stands, like the cedar and hemlock that once grew on Sherman's river pasture, may have burned once every few hundred years: these stands can be said to be "fire-initiated." Ecosystems as diverse and widely separated as the loblolly pine forests of the southeastern U.S., the tallgrass prairies of Manitoba and the upper U.S. Midwest, and eastern Oregon's sagebrush/juniper, have been historically maintained by fire. Some fires seem to have the ability to keep ecosystems on track; other fires, usually the hotter ones, can permanently convert one type of ecosystem to another.

The idea that some ecosystems are fire-maintained — requiring occasional fire to maintain health and proper species balance — is a difficult one to accept. For us, landscape is a construct, a fixed and enduring piece of literature. We assemble landscape in our heads, from shreds of ancient mythology, half-remembered Disney movies, romantic yearnings, cultural assumptions, primal landscapes and genetic anachronisms. The final product of our mental assembling may not have much to do with the actual landscape itself. We approach real landscapes through a set of cultural or literary stereotypes — Elysian fields, forbidding forests, brooding coastlines, English gardens, monotonous prairies, harsh deserts and so on. Like the primal landscape and the remembered landscape, the perceived landscape is not supposed to change. It is no wonder we resist the idea of ecosystems being adapted to or needing fire, when the very essence of fire is its ability to radically change the landscape.

History is a useful check on our constructs of perception. Trees, fortunately, contain their own historical archive. Young conifers that are burned severely, but not killed, can develop a "fire scar" of exposed inner wood. Every subsequent fire scorches the exposed bark edge around the margin of the scar, leaving a permanent record in the annual growth rings of the tree. When the stand is logged or thinned, the rings can be analysed in the older, fire-scarred veterans. The interval between fire scars, determined by counting annual growth rings, determines the "fire periodicity," which can vary from an extreme of two or three years in the driest ponderosa pine sites to four or five hundred years in cool, wet forests.

A colleague and I analysed the cross-section of a 400-year-old fire-scarred western larch that came out of the Rocky Mountain Trench, near the headwaters of the Columbia River. I could pick out 1807, the year that the explorer David Thompson would have, according to his journals, passed within sight of the tree. I could see a massive fire scar from 1932, a memento of the forest fires that ravaged the area in the Dirty Thirties. As I familiarized myself with the broad, sanded slab, it gradually transformed itself into a complex bio-historical graph, whose X and Y co-ordinates were not abstract points in geometric space, but whorled and varying growth rings, etched here and there by blackened, intrusive fire scars. Tree ring and fire scar analysis are tools of the emerging discipline of "landscape archaeology," which may help us learn to think about nature as a dynamic, instead of as a constant.

Many western forest dendrochronologies show a "spike" of more frequent fire activity from about 1880 to 1940, as newly arrived railroads belched sparks, miners burned mountainsides to better see rock formations, loggers left huge, flammable slashpiles, nobody was very careful and some people simply liked to see things burn. Organized forest fire suppression began in the U.S. around 1930, and in Canada around 1937. Fire frequency in both countries dropped dramatically after those dates.

Pinus ponderosa is the quintessential fire-adapted tree of the western forests. It has the look of a huge bonsai: twisted, drooping branches, with upswept branchlets. The trunk of a mature tree is a massive, even-diametered column that tapers suddenly and dramatically at the top. This tree literally defines a certain kind of dry, rocky Western Interior scene, from the central interior of British Columbia all the way to Mexico City and east as far as the Black Hills of North Dakota. It is found in dry interior valleys and up to 3,000 metres in the Rockies and Sierras. With the curious exception of Alberta, the western traveller has the ponderosa as a constant companion. Standing dead snags of the durable ponderosa are highly sought after by cavity-nesting birds. Lewis and Clark first described the tree, but it was the Irish botanist David Douglas who gave the tree its resonant name, which is derived from Latin and means "ponderous," referring to the massive trunk. If Douglas had worked in the 1960s instead of the 1830s, he might have called it "heavy pine."

Ponderosa is associated with wisdom: in Spanish, one of the meanings of the term is circumspect, grave. Many of the aboriginal cultures of the Western Interior had the tradition of the Council Grove: when a tribe had a particularly weighty matter to discuss, they would hold their meeting under the lofty canopy of a group of mature ponderosas. The landscape of large, well-spaced trees with grass underneath is associated with contemplation even in this culture, and is carefully cultivated in hundreds of university campuses.

When I ask friends and colleagues to describe their primal,

reference landscape for me, several have responded with images that include ponderosa pine. The veteran ponderosa pine's bark is tawny and fissured, its irregular branches start high up the trunk, and the long needles are arranged in sprays. Cones of the ponderosa are pineapple-shaped, and open when mature. The tree's neighbors are sagebrush, grassland and desert along the lower, drier edges of its habitat. As moisture and elevation increase, it cohabits with Douglas-fir, larch, lodgepole, aspen, juniper and pinyon. The species seems to have a penchant for dramatic and lightning-prone settings. It is a tree that swims in memory, and surfaces in dreams.

Listen to Rebecca Ketcham, a settler who described the ponderosa pine forests of eastern Oregon's Blue Mountains country in 1853:

> After dinner, when we had ascended the first hill, we looked back on the country we had passed through. I can almost say I never saw anything more beautiful, the [Grande Ronde] river winding about through the ravines, the forests so different from anything I have seen before. The country all through is burnt over, so often there is not the least underbrush, but the grass grows thick and beautiful. It is now ripe and yellow and in the spaces between the groves (which are large and many) looks like fields of grain ripened, ready for the harvest.

To stand in a healthy forest of these trees is a particular kind of honor. The landscape of the healthy ponderosa pine forest is that of parkland or savannah. It is the psychological equivalent of the old African forest-grassland fringes where our species was born. Massive and elegant, ponderosa trunks lead upward to open crowns frequented by crows and eagles. Shafts of undiluted sunlight drift all the way down through the canopy, to splash on bunchgrass. Lightning-scarred veterans and the standing-dead — some more like icons than trees — have twisted, retrorse branches. Rock in these forests is never far away, harboring swifts, alligator lizards and the occasional rattlesnake. The canopy does close in the very best growing sites, but it does so far above head height. It is difficult to enter a healthy ponderosa pine forest without wishing for a saddle horse. Heated afternoon air will stink of pine resin and the sound the wind makes as it moves through the upper canopy is like that of no other forest. The sound speaks of freedom, of the onward rush of seasons. John Muir noted this, saying "of all pines, this one gives forth the finest music to the winds."

One of the many commensal, or mutually beneficial, partnerships ponderosa maintains is with the grasses that grow underneath it. Dry grasses provide the fuels that carry light surface fires through these open forests, killing most of the young pine and fir seedlings that have established. Dry forests must find a delicate balance between the survival of mature trees and the recruitment of new seedlings, and the ponderosa forest uses fire to effect that balance.

To describe a phenomenon that operates in cycles, the trick is to know where to start. In the case of the fire-adapted ponderosa pine forest, a good point of entry is in a middle-aged stand, ten years after the most recent fire. A wet, El Niño spring three years prior has created a flush of new tree seedlings, some of which are the sun-loving ponderosa, others the more shade-tolerant Douglas-fir. Dry grass, old needles and dead branches have begun to accumulate on the ground. A July electrical storm moves through the area, and a lightning bolt strikes the dead crown of an old ponderosa vet, literally blowing it apart. Burning bits of wood fall to the ground, and the dry grass underneath catches fire. Upslope winds push the fire and it races through the grass and dead needles, lingering wherever it finds more substantial fuel — tree seedlings, shrubs, and dead wood. Occasionally the flames reach high enough to scorch the lower branches of adult ponderosas, and scattered Douglas-fir and lodgepole adults are actually consumed. In a few hours the fire is all over, leaving what looks like devastation. The ground is black, stumps and downed trees smolder, shrubs and tree seedlings are charred.

The spring following the fire, perennial grasses come up early. Their belowground growing points were protected from the fire's lethal temperatures, and the additional sunshine coming through the thinned tree canopy warms still-blackened soil, coaxing them to grow. Saskatoon shrubs sprout from the bases of fire-killed stems, and the previously sealed seeds of Ceanothus, a fire-dependent shrub, are now able to germinate.

Deer and elk move in to the area, attracted by new and succulent forage. A few standing dead trees blow down, beginning their fertile conversion to insect and small mammal habitat, sunning places for lizards, and finally organic matter for the forest soil. The mature ponderosas that remain enjoy a holiday: fewer trees means their desperate search for water is now not quite so desperate, and the water they seek now contains an extra spritz of nitrogen liberated from the bodies of their fallen comrades. Dendrochronologies of fire-scarred trees often show a period of rapid growth after a fire event.

Fires like these never cover the ground completely; they will always miss a patch here that is too wet, or another one there that hasn't enough fuel to carry fire. So as a healthy ponderosa pine forest ages, it does so as an increasingly diverse mosaic of even-aged patches, a habit that drives forest planners crazy.

If such a ten-year fire cycle is suppressed for sixty years, a whole new dynamic takes over. The flush of even-aged new seedlings grows up to become a dense, even-aged forest underneath the original forest. Open grasslands become treed grasslands, treed grasslands become open forests, and open forests become closed forests, each site hosting far more trees than it can possibly sustain. Fire-intolerant, shade-tolerant Douglas-fir often becomes the dominant tree under conditions of fire suppression. As the fir trees mature, competition for light, water and nutrients becomes intense. Individual tree growth slows down a little bit every year until it reaches a standstill, leaving dense, even-aged, stagnated thickets of what are crudely known as "peckerpole" Douglas-fir. Meanwhile, the relic ponderosa pines and larches struggle to keep their heads above the fir canopy, like drowning men.

Soon the fir thickets become biological deserts, shading the ground so completely that no grass, shrub or wildflower can grow. If local children are a certain age and weight however, and the trees are just thick enough to climb but thin enough to still bend, these thickets do have a use. The children can climb the firs until they bend, then grab the next tree and then the next, swinging through the forest like temperate Tarzans.

Ingrown fir thickets have a dark side. They contain large

amounts of flammable fuel, arranged in "ladder" fashion from the ground right up through the canopy. Ground fires that move into fir thickets quickly become explosive, unpredictable crown fires. Many of the fires that raged across Washington, British Columbia, Idaho and Montana were of this nature.

To understand how various tree species respond to fire, we would ideally have a neat linear scale of The Fire Sensitivity of Certain Forest Trees, which might start with the very flammable cedars, work through Douglas-fir to juniper and western larch, and then finally to the tough ponderosa pine. This ideal scheme is complicated by the lodgepole. Lodgepole and its cousin, jack pine, have tightly closed cones that won't even release their seed until they are heated by fire, yet the trees themselves burn like roman candles. Nature never seems to be very keen on linear, predictable relationships.

After a hot, stand-destroying forest fire, the cones of lodgepole pine release vast quantities of seed that will quickly grow up to become a fire-prone lodgepole forest. If no subsequent fire attacks this new forest, the mountain pine beetle will eventually kill it. This tree is an ecological chess player that makes early pawn sacrifices, and is able to think so many moves ahead that it sees the game from an entirely different perspective. Lodgepole is also the philosopher: it cares not for the survival of the individual. Its quest seems not to be for dominance of its species over other tree species, but rather for the survival of ecosystems that contain opportunities for lodgepole.

It is early spring as I write this, the Easter long weekend. Snow has left the lower valleys of the Kootenays, the sun is out, and people clad in overalls and gloves are busy in their yards and acreages. All day Saturday they haul branches, rake leaves and so on. Late Saturday afternoon the first tentative fire is started, just a modest pile of leaves or perhaps the remains of last season's rampant quackgrass. Soon others take up the call. By Sunday afternoon, several smokes are visible, and on Monday, the air all over town is pungent with the particular stink of burning grass. Ditches and roadsides are burned. Overgrown fencelines are burned. Grassy hillsides are burned. Staggy old apple trees are cut down and burned.

Along the way, the neighbor's painted fence will get scorched, the tires on someone else's boat trailer catch fire, and there is talk that some old barn up the valley fell victim to a well-intentioned grass fire.

Common wisdom has it that this kind of spring burning has an ethnic origin. On the prairies it is ascribed to the Indians; here in the Kootenays it is supposed to be a habit of the Doukhobors. As a student of burning, a pyrecologist if you will, I can confirm that the urge to burn the landscape is present in every ethnic group, and has been for some time. African evidence of the human use of fire goes back 1.4 million years. As Stephen Pyne says, "fire belongs with other critical acquisitions by *Homo erectus*, including speech, stone tools, and an explosive growth in brain size." When I burnt down the cedar tree in Sherman's river pasture, I was not acting out of context for my species, regardless of what Mr. Sherman and the county authorities thought. In big city folk the urge is suppressed, but give a person some land, enough rainfall to produce carryover vegetation, and a sunny weekend in early spring, and the urge to burn will arise.

In aboriginal North America, fires were started for defence, for agriculture, for game management, for access, for insect control, even for reducing willow stem diameter to produce better basket-making material. Here is a typical description of the fire-starting habit, as described by a colonist in Massachusetts in 1632:

> The [indians] are accustomed to set fire of the country in all places where they come, and to burn it twice a year, vixe, at the spring, and at the fall of the leafe. The reason that moves them to do so, is because it would be otherwise so overgrown with underweedes that it would all be a coppice wood, and the people could not be able in any wise to passe through the country out of a beaten path.

Landscape ecologists are now faced with the speculation: if this anthropogenic fire is present on the landscape for a long enough period, say a thousand years or more, does it then become part of the "natural" background that ecosystems respond to? We know that some ecosystems, if not most of them, have in one fashion or another genetically adapted themselves to periodic fires. Are humans, along with lightning, part of this periodicity? Is burning one of the few "natural" things we can do?

All this is not to romanticize fire. Excessively hot fires can wreck soils, permanently alter forest succession, and threaten lives. Old-timers of nearly every rural family — from both the prairies and the mountains — have stories to tell of the terrors and near-misses of wildfire. Fire control will always have a major role in our forests and rural areas. The irony is that developers love to build expensive suburban homes in the most fire-prone ecosystems — those picturesque stands of ponderosa pine, juniper, sagebrush, and chaparral that are found from Penticton to Flagstaff, from Cranbrook to Bend. I have vivid childhood memories of such fires in the shrub chaparral of southern California. My father and other men from our ordinary Pasadena neighborhood would be drafted to build fire lines around the hillside mansions of the wealthy, who had chosen to build in the foothills of the Sierra Madres, one of the more fire-prone ecosystems in the world.

An understanding of fire ecology will help put intense fire years, like 1994, into perspective. It is probably too much to ask of TV newscasters, who dearly love disasters, to go beyond the mere size of the forest fire and the number of houses it consumed, to report on the more central questions of the natural fire return rate of the area, the amount of ingrowth, the level of fuel loading, and the time elapsed since the last fire.

The challenge for the rest of us is to recognize the ecological need for fire on certain landscapes, to understand fire's every technical and biological nuance, and to reintroduce this wild, random event into the densely settled and closely managed context of today. Not the way I did in Dungeness, but carefully, with an understanding of the contradictions inherent in planning for randomness, and in artificially re-creating a natural event. To do that will take a certain amount of humility.

☉

7

Primal

A POET FRIEND OF MINE has a theory about children. She says there is a period in their lives when they bond with a particular home landscape, and the image of that landscape stays with them through their lifetime, as a profound psychological imprint. I think I believe this theory; in fact I can imagine such imprinting occurring within a single childhood afternoon, as familiar sounds and smells and light entwine and expand to a kind of sensory maximum. The receptive child then looks up momentarily from a round stone or a creek, feels a light, emotional detonation somewhere within the rib cage, and is imprinted forever.

This primal landscape, as my friend calls it, then forms part of that grand dream we call "home," and becomes a semiconscious reference against which the individual will then compare all other landscapes. She cites the case of her own grown children, the oldest who spent part of his childhood in southeast Asia, where the family lived for a time, and the two others who grew up entirely in Canada. The oldest has retained a strong hankering for lushness and humidity, to the point of walking through summer rainstorms, a trait the other two children do not share. Discovering places similar to the primal landscape will naturally evoke strong positive feelings. My wife grew up in a seaside community near Seattle and, even though she has no real desire to live near the ocean now, she finds the smell of tideflats and the sound of waves breaking at night to be urgent, compelling messages. It is as if certain sights, sounds and smells bypass the senses and speak directly to her being. Perhaps we do carry around some fossil genetic coding for an enhanced memory of the natal or childhood place.

Dissimilar landscapes, ones that contrast strongly with the primal landscape, can generate unease, even active disgust. We all know of stories of prairie dwellers being unable to cope with the claustrophobia of mountains and forests, or of newcomers to the prairies being driven to distraction by the immensity of sky and the lack of relief.

The finality of my friend's theory is such that one does not want to be caught without a primal landscape, but I confess to not having one. Most people's certainties seem to be my ambiguities. I do have childhood memories of rolling California annual grasslands, studded with eucalyptus and tickbrush, but my father was a typical 1950s sunbelt boomer, and we never stayed in one place very long. I think whatever did imprint on me simply evaporated, due to mobility and forgetfulness. Even the landscapes themselves are now gone, ravaged by freeways and housing developments from Pasadena to Santa Rosa.

So I have always travelled a lot, trying on landscapes. That was what I was doing when, as a young man travelling in South America, I felt a belated primal landscape detonation. I was on a gaudy, outlaw bus of the kind that haunts the roads of rural Colombia, grinding up over the mountains of the Cordillera Occidental towards Cali, on the coastal plain. I had not expected anything out of the ordinary of the trip, just the usual small farms, plantations and bush. The mountain pass we went over was much higher than I had ever imagined though, and the switchback road finally settled out, at 12,000 feet, onto a bizarre and lonely plateau. The bus stopped at a rough colono farmhouse along the road for coffee and repairs, and I had a few hours to walk in what will forever remain as one of the most exotic landscapes I have ever seen; that of high, cold jungle. Low oxygen, saturated soils, high precipitation, no seasons, little sun, cold, and probably eons of stability. Paramo, the Colombians call it; the land on top. Everything around me was strange and raw, right down to the boards of the colono's house. A few sheep belonging to the colono stood motionless in the rain, looking absolutely stunned. Tall, sepulchral "frailejon" cactus plants[1] dotted the hummocky plateau. Their twisted stems were barren, but the very tops of these plants were crowned with long, spikelike leaves. The ground underfoot was spongy, like that of rainforest. In the distance a steep, cone-shaped hill thrust up precipitously through the plateau, and its sides were clothed in dense forest instead of the strange cactus. A waterfall gushed down one side of the hill, fed apparently, by the clouds that raked continuously over its summit. I wandered further afield, half-expecting the frailejon to respond to my presence somehow, by folding up like sensitive-plants, or by venting despondent sighs. The bus and even the reason for the trip to Cali suddenly became of no consequence. Like the misplaced chick, I felt myself strongly attracted to this dramatically foreign landscape. I have carried the memory of that paramo with me for many years, as one primal candidate, the exotic one. Seeing paramo was like finally arriving at a landscape that one had visited over and over in dreams.

Years later, I had the chance to read about and understand something of paramo's ecology. For example, the great differences between the plateau and hillside vegetation came from the ability of well-drained hillside soils to support tree growth, whereas the waterlogged plateau soils acted much like arctic permafrost, supporting only scrubby, surface-rooted vegetation. But learning these things took nothing away from the paramo's sense of mystery. I learned also that Alexander von Humboldt and the French botanist Boussingault explored these realms in the 1840s. Those two scientific adventurers no doubt revelled in paramo's strangeness as well, and probably used it as a marker of their distance from the decadent salons of Europe.

The idea of bonding with the paramo landscape seemed to me like the very definition of romance. By somehow attaching myself to that landscape, I could partake of its remoteness, its exotic nature, its purity. Paramo could become an extension of my personality and, if I met it cleanly and strongly enough, it could nourish me.

As I look back on that time, I see both the weakness and the strength of those feelings.

Travelling in search of the belated landscape bond, or the lost imprint, is risky. To seek a substitute primal landscape means telescoping an intuitive childhood event into the self-aware, ambiguous state of adulthood, and I am not at all sure that can be done. There can be consequences, as Will James proved. Nevertheless, the quest for primal terrain is the leitmotif of a certain kind of rootless traveller, one who continuously sorts through landscapes in search of the right one to bolt a loosened existence to. The landscape voyeur finds a certain satisfaction in dissatisfaction.

As an adult, it takes a long time to learn a set of local landscapes, to begin to call a region "home." To measure that process is to sense the actual ticking of one's lifespan. By the time the learning is done, it is often time to leave and to place a new form of ownership on those landscapes, as the place where you are from.

Those with firmly imprinted landscapes also travel, either to reinforce the "rightness" of the imprinted landscape, cultivating the illusion that they have actually chosen it, or they travel for the arousal offered by safely and momentarily trying on some contrasting, alien landscape, as if it were a kind of mask. Finding individuals whose imprinted landscape is still their home landscape is a rarity now, due to mobility and the dominance of cities. Those folks whose inner, imprinted landscapes coincide with their outer ones don't travel much, and when they do, they frequently bring a jug of local drinking water with them.

Searching for a primal landscape has been one motive for my travel, but there are other motives as well. Travel is in some sense an illusion, a headgame, an excuse for seeing the same things I see at home, but in different ways. Even Colombian paramo is really no more unique and remote and exotic than the cedar-hemlock forests of my home in the Kootenays, and that colono sheep farmer on the paramo probably went to sleep at night dreaming of the romantic Canadian forests. Walking the humdrum home landscapes now and then, pretending that one has just newly arrived there on a visit from far away, is probably a good exercise.

The primal landscape imprint — and possibly, the lack of it — provides a platform for other, more conscious bonds with nature. John Muir and the Sierra, Farley Mowat and the Arctic, Thoreau and Walden Pond, Lawren Harris with northern Ontario, Emily Carr with the British Columbia coast, and so on. None of these people grew up in the places they came to love, but they certainly had the capacity for a kind of passionate adoption.

Natural landscapes offer intimacy, but they can also help remind us of the insignificance of our species, provided we remove our hands, however briefly, from the powerful lever of technology. The sense of insignificance that nature can provide is liberating; without the reassuring vastness of geologic time and space, we are simply alone, with our brief and gnawing consciousness.

However strong a landscape bond may be in the individual, it is not shared by the society in which we live, in spite of mythologies to the contrary. Development continuously erodes the possibilities. Socially we denigrate strong attachment to natural landscape as an essentially feminine trait, unless it is coupled with an equally strong desire to extract natural resources from it. Landscape bonds are often kept private, like embarrassing birthmarks. Mainstream society's nature ethic seems to be far more influenced by the male stance of dominance rather than the more female trait of attachment, probably for economic reasons. Rational activities on the land are assumed to be only those which generate monetary return. But if the concept of landscape imprinting is accepted, then the feminine and the maternal come as an integral part of the psychological package, since any form of imprinting involves a mother. Explicit social acknowledgment of our nonmaterial needs for natural landscape, which are feminine and positively so, will be a breakthrough for all of us.

Landscape and the feminine are connected in other ways. Both are vessels for our conception of beauty. The wild graces and symmetries that originally defined beauty for us were first seen in women and then, in the next breath, transferred to natural landscapes. Legions of painters and photographers have honored this connection. Walt Whitman put it this way:

> As I see my soul reflected in nature;
> As I see through a mist, one with inexpressible completeness
>   and beauty,
> See the bent head, and arms folded over the breast — the
>   female I see."

Paradoxically, female breasts symbolize all that is right — and wrong — with our relationship to nature. Organs of intimacy, generosity and abundance, they are also highly subject to industrial carcinogens. Researchers are finding that a whole range of chlorine-based compounds — from DDT to dioxin — mimic the structure of human estrogen. The estrogen receptors on the surfaces of breast cells, innocent of our realities of technology and pollution, usher these alien compounds inside, where they can accumulate and trigger breast cancer. It is somehow very fitting that the female breast has become the bell-wether, the mine canary, for our petrochemical lifestyle.

I think the flush I felt in first seeing the paramo was in part an erotic flush. Psychologists tell us that several sexual fantasies per day are normal for both men and women, but they say nothing about the landscape fantasies, which I indulge in at about the same rate. Often the landscape and the sexual fantasies get mixed together. That to me seems natural, since the two pursuits share mutual concerns of privacy, shape, and feverish exploration. Visually I calibrate women's hips against mine, and visually I calibrate landscapes against my armspread, my capacity for embrace. There is a level of spirituality in women and in natural landscapes that I count on to move me beyond my own often mundane and corporeal levels. If this spirituality is actually an illusion, then for me it is a very necessary one.

Many other landscapes have presented themselves to me since the paramo, each making their claim before a yearning psyche. The harsher, lonelier landscapes seem particularly attractive, resonating with my own solitary aspects. I now have a number of ambiguous landscape attachments and I am cursed, as one colleague put it, with the ability to like every place I get to know. Meanwhile, my friend's theory of primal bonds sits quietly on the horizon, implacable. I know she will grant me the right to search for a primal landscape. She is a poet, and poets in general seem sympathetic to quests. So I will continue accumulating this clutter of geographical experience, these failed and romantic imprints, but I doubt, given the fatal nature of her theory, that anyone gets a second chance at that first childhood bond.

---

1. *Espeletia* sp.

8

Ground Truth

A PRAIRIE RE-EXPLORATION took me back through the File Hills of southern Saskatchewan, where I had worked many years before. The landscape of grain farms, coulees and bush triggered a rush of long-dormant memories of days on the Indian reserves in those hills. I let the memories come on, mindful of the trap of nostalgia, curious to filter those experiences through my current sensibilities, and knowing I had several hours of driving time before I stopped for the night.

This latest gadget in my life was called a planimeter. It came nestled in a velvet-lined box and was encrusted with dials, measuring scales and various adjusting screws. A scientific instrument like this was precisely the kind of thing my ancestors had given me a genetic weakness for. I tried to tell George how this new piece of technology could save us days and days of tramping around, measuring reserve fields. George was hostile though, and would not pay attention as I put the gorgeous little planimeter on top of a brand new aerial photograph and began to trace out a field.

"Actually, you can't help being wrong on your measurements," George said, "since you're using those damn photographs. And if that's Fred Poitras' field you are trying to measure, forget it. I know that field. It's a Texas quarter because Fred farms the road allowance, so there's 170 acres total. His field was 110 acres to start with, so you subtract that, then there's the ten acres of sloughs and also that fifteen-acre pasture in the corner that his kids use for calf roping, and you subtract those, too. And you remember we told the contractor to leave five acres of bush around Fred's house. So you subtract those five and there you go, what's left over is thirty acres of bush, and that's how much the contractor must have cleared. It's just simple math, Gayton."

I ground my teeth quietly, and kept on tracing. A lavish prairie sunset spilled through the windows of the drab agricultural extension office, where George, Anwar and I had gathered after a day's work. George was serious, but there were tiny laugh wrinkles in the corners of his eyes. He lived for calculation, and good arguments.

Acreage measurements had become vitally important to us. As the native farmers we worked with expanded their operations, we hired contractors on their behalf to bulldoze and clear new farmland for them. In the old days when Indian Affairs was in charge of this work, some of the contractors had gotten away with murder by padding their acreage claims, knowing that no one would actually go out to walk the fields and check on them. Not any more. In the slow dance of learning to work with each other, George and I found total agreement on the sanctity of measuring these newly cleared fields and not paying the contractors a single nickel more than their due. Getting accurate acreage figures became like a mission: we would spend days tramping over the fertile chaos of roots and soil, measuring and remeasuring, working behind the big cats as they sheared off aspen and jack pine. It took a lot of time, and a lot of approximation.

"Fred's field isn't a fair test of this system," I said finally, "because you already know that field. Once I figure this planimeter out, we can use it to take measurements of any field, right off these photographs. And it could even be a field you haven't seen before."

George snorted. "And what about that estimate you made on Harold Keesekoot's field? I guess that little machine of yours doesn't know the difference between 40 acres and 400."

He had me on that point. But there I was, the new kid, and George had forty years of reserve farming experience. I still couldn't tell an acre if it fell on me, and George not only knew most of the fields we measured, but had actually farmed some of them on cropshare. He talked about them like they were members of his family. The planimeter and the photographs were going to be my way of getting professional parity with George. But my maiden estimate, on Harold's land, was a wonderfully precise disaster, right out to the third decimal place.

George leaned back in his chair, stretched out his legs and thumped his big cowboy boots down on the corner of my desk. He was beginning to enjoy this, I could tell. George, Anwar and I had been together long enough to know that each put in a full day working with the farmers, and we had come to see these occasional sessions after work as a kind of payoff.

"Okay," I said, resuming the argument. "I admit I've got to do some fine-tuning on my planimeter technique. But look, some of our walking estimates could be way off, and you know it."

George denied that statement as if he were under oath.

"What about when mud gets caked all over the measuring wheel, and makes it bigger," I countered. That's going to throw our numbers out of whack. Or what about when we start walking towards a field corner that we can't see because there's a hill right in the middle of the field. There's no way we can guarantee we're walking in a straight line towards the corner."

George was not even listening; he had turned to Anwar and started talking about a farm loan the two of them were working on. I knew he would answer eventually; this was his way of letting me know that my arguments did not merit an immediate response.

Turning back to me finally, George pointed to the photographs on my desk by motioning with the toe of his big boot.

"I tell you those damn things are no good. How could some bloody pilot from Edmonton know anything about this land?

He'd be lost in five minutes if he ever came on the reserve. Let alone be able to walk across a half-section that's just been broke. And that machine," he said, more for Anwar's benefit than mine, "that machine of yours is nothing but a toy for grown-ups."

"Ah, now I see. You don't like all this technology because it makes things too easy."

George responded that my biggest problem was that I couldn't add figures in my head, a statement that had a grain of truth to it.

Getting accurate measurements on some of the newly broken fields had been a real challenge. Indian fields, because of complex hereditary ownership systems and because of an enduring respect for bush, were never square, or even rectangular. Instead they were complex serpentines, trapezoids, and irregular polygons. Reserves had none of the geometric, easily measured landscape of the white man's prairies. Indian farmers tended to stay clear of sloughs with good muskrat, worked their way around old sweat lodges, and kept their cultivators at a respectful distance from sacred ground. Once we were measuring on Little Black Bear, George's own reserve, and he took me aside to a narrow grove of aspen that wound through the field. There in the bush, half-buried in aspen leaves, was the single gravestone of one of his relatives. I brushed the leaves aside; below the man's name was the date of his death in France — 1914 — and below that was inscribed a single word, one that spoke volumes. "SAPPER," it said. We went back to our work without comment.

Our standard way to measure a field was to divide it up into a series of blocks, rectangles and triangles, and then walk the perimeter of each one, pushing a measuring wheel in front of us. The wheel was made in Cederholm, Texas, and had a handle with a little counter on it. The wheel measured six-feet-six inches in circumference, and every revolution moved the counter ahead by one. Six-feet-six was a number of pure Anglo-Saxon mystery, since it related mathematically, by obscure multipliers, to the Chain, and the Chain to the Acre. Rods and Furlongs were separate.

I would puzzle over these curious, quirky units as we

walked behind the wheel, wondering if they could be traced back to some ancient rites of mensuration at Stonehenge or some other mysterious place. I could visualize hooded figures pacing off sacred distances in the dark of night, measuring barleycorns and knuckle joints. Torches would flare against carefully placed stone slabs. There would be chanting, and sometime around sunrise, a sheep or goat would be sacrificed. Forever after, farmers and fieldmen pay secret homage by muttering about chains-to-acres and rods-to-furlongs. And here *we* were, deep into the twentieth century, still thinking it was all science. Meanwhile George would be working and reworking numbers in his head, adding up the little blocks and rectangles and triangles. Half a quarter here, add two forties, subtract ten for the woodlot, call that borrow pit two acres, and so on. Sometimes the mosquitoes were fierce.

We were still measuring on foot, balancing George's direct-intuitive against my pseudorational, when someone told me that the whole region had been recorded in aerial photographs, and there was a device called a planimeter that one could use to measure land area right on the photograph. I persuaded Head Office to let me buy the measuring device and a set of photos.

A quick look at the manual revealed that you placed the planimeter right on top of the photograph, held the weighted base steady in one place, and slowly moved the jointed measuring arm, capturing sloughs and bluffs and fields. The central part of the machine had a set of tiny number wheels, like an odometer. As you moved along the edge of a field with the arm, the number wheels would spin, slow or reverse direction obediently. When you had traced the field all the way back to your starting point, the final figures on the number wheels could be converted into acreage, again by an obscure formula. I had no idea what actually happened inside the little machine, but was naturally attracted to it.

George finally slid his boots off my desk and sprawled them across our cramped office. We all felt a bit like overfed housecats in the warm sunlight. Then George came back at me with his big gun, his most trenchant criticism, the fact that photographs flatten out the hills that are so painfully evident to the farmer on his tractor. That to him was a most damnable fact, and he was eloquent about the three-dimensional nature of farmland. Anwar was obviously enjoying this, I had to admit I was too, as the whole argument began to slide off into play. We made an odd trio, the quiet Egyptian, the older Indian farmer and the young pseudorational. It was clear from the first day we started working together that any friendships would first be subject to performance; each one of us had something to prove. So far we had been doing well. We all managed to do some violence to nearly everyone's stereotype, and that was a help. Head Office was a hundred kilometres away, and that was helpful, too.

George stood up to go.

"Look Gayton," he said. "We're settling up with Holovaty and Sons tomorrow on that big clearing contract on Ministawin. You bring those damn photographs and that little machine of yours along."

I was surprised. Old Metro Holovaty was our toughest contractor, and the farmers told us he had taken Indian Affairs to the cleaners a couple of times. Whenever we negotiated with him, Metro was always flanked by his two mountainous sons, who were usually flanked in turn by their mountainous, rumbling D8 Caterpillar tractors. The Holovaty clan's idea of contract negotiation was to spread the maps and the contract out on the muddy treads of an idling D8, and then yell at us over the sound of the engine. They moved in an atmosphere of diesel, and the boys seemed to genuinely enjoy knocking trees over with their big machines.

"Jeez, George," I said, genuinely surprised, "I didn't think I would ever convert you so easily."

George Belanger leaned over my desk and casually moved one of the weights holding down my stack of unrolled photographs. Instantly they re-rolled themselves into a tight little bundle. My precious planimeter was inside, along with several pencils, a notepad, and my calculator.

"Just bring 'em along, Gayton. Old Man Holovaty will be so impressed with your scientific stuff that he won't dare pad his acreage claim. You just baffle them with your bullshit and we'll use my numbers."

He left. Anwar smiled and shook two fingers quickly, like he had just burnt them. We listened to George's big boots echoing down the drab green stairwell. He would be heading to Regina to spend the rest of the evening at the track, working more numbers. Anwar stood up to go too, since there wasn't a lot left to say.

I stayed on, saying I had to make a few phone calls. When Anwar was gone, I went out to the confectionery and bought a big bag of taco chips, and then came back to the planimeter instruction book. An hour later, I had it; ground truth. A fundamental that I had missed on my first reading.

Ground truth turned out to be a minor revelation, a good concept with some poetry to it. Find two specific landmarks on the ground that can also be seen in the photograph, and then measure the distance between them, once in the photograph, and once on the ground. Fix those two distances into a ratio, like an inch on the photograph equals a mile on the ground. Suddenly two independent objects, the little quadrant of real earth and the photographic image of it, now have a bond and a fixed relation to one another, a benchmark, a ground truth.

I could now verify my photographic artifacts, my representations of reality, in reality itself. And by inference, all the other parts of that artifact would bear the same ratio to the real world. The measure from the slough to the edge of the aspen bluff then, or from the grid road out to the working corrals, is meaningful. Those humble distances are a leg up into the universe.

I felt illuminated, and couldn't wait to tell George about ground truth. I could use analogies to explain it, like what a person says can be ground-truthed by what they do. Scientific theories can be ground-truthed by known facts. There was even a ground truth for what we were doing: the success of an agricultural development program could be ground-truthed over the scratched formica of a beginning farmer's kitchen table.

I thought about how the next day at Ministawin might go.

We had walked every inch of that clearing project, and Metro would get paid for exactly the amount that he had done. George would have the figures, and I would have the supporting hardware. I could show Metro the velvet-lined box, and perhaps mention ground truth. George might even buy in to the concept if he thought it could gain us an edge in negotiations with Metro.

Finally I put the planimeter and manual back into the box, and closed up the office for the night. My sneakers were muffled in the stairwell compared to the sound of George's boots, which echoed through the building as he came and went. I realized that George Belanger was a kind of ground truth for me. The friendship of this particular human being was my benchmark, a friendship that could lift me into the world of others.

The File Hills were now far behind me, and my eastward journey continued. Prairie landscapes slowly gave way to aspen parkland as the Manitoba border approached. I pulled the van off onto a side road and got out to stretch my legs in a bush pasture. Soon I was wandering along narrow lanes of natural grassland as they wound between the great rounded clumps of aspen. This prairie tree reproduces exclusively by suckering, so the trees of each separate clump, or bluff, as prairie folk call them, can be genetically identical to each other. A biologist friend had told me that the largest living organism was not a sperm whale or a subterranean fungus, but a huge aspen clone somewhere in Utah. If there was any self-doubt connected to the memories of those File Hills days, it would be about the amount of aspen bush that I helped convert to farmland. I do seem to have a talent for manufacturing my own paradoxes.

A coyote returned me to the present by mincing delicately between the aspen bluffs in front of me. I seem to live within the three points of a strongly skewed triangle: rarely in nature, occasionally in the body, and mostly in the head. Mental life seems to be the most compelling. Walks like this one often leave me more firmly planted on the point of interior consciousness than on the point of nature itself.

On a whim I changed direction, to see if I could track the coyote into the tangled aspen.

9

The Image and the Breaks

I HAVE A LONG-STANDING HABIT of taking slide photographs of natural landscapes. I seldom bring them out to look at them after taking them, but the making of these photographic records seems important to me, for some nebulous reasons of posterity.

My re-explorations so far had been by actual travel and by memory; examining my slide collection seemed to be a valid third method. I decided to kill two birds with one stone and revisit the landscapes of these slides at the same time as I labelled them. So I assembled a few years' worth of photographs on a light table and began writing minute descriptions and locations on the plastic slide frames. Many of the slides fell naturally into small groups, with one or two long shots of a particular place, followed by close-ups of the same locale, showing some plant or rock formation. I became quite absorbed, trying to see patterns and meanings in the kinds of landscapes that I took pictures of. Then I came upon a single slide of a landscape I did not recognize. I put it into a viewer to take a closer look. A river ran along the bottom foreground of the picture, and a long, barren hillside formed the background. A few scrubby, almost blackish trees dotted the hillside. The slide's coloration was so severe — black trees, pale yellow hillside, silver water — that I wondered for a moment if I was looking at some kind of negative image. What dry and forgotten corner of the Western Interior could this be? I began a methodical scan of the entire image, looking for some scrap of recognition that would link it to my travels.

Where was this place and how did I get a photograph of it? First I wondered if someone else's slide could have gotten mixed in with mine, but my own name was boldly printed right on the slide's frame, and its number was right in sequence with the rest of the shots from that roll of film. Could someone else have taken the picture? I couldn't remember ever loaning my camera to anyone; cameras are usually private things, and mine was no exception. A slight shiver ran through me as I realized I had never seen this landscape before.

Over the next few days I worked through all other logical possibilities for the slide's existence, and found none whatsoever. Then a curious thing happened; I began to contemplate the possibility that the slide was of an imaginary landscape. The idea of a landscape that was purely mental, or at least nonphysical in origin, suddenly became much more interesting than the actual mechanism of its arrival in my camera. As a child, I had recurring dreams of a very particular imaginary landscape, one of upturned, charred stumps, whose chaotic roots reached high into the sky above me. That landscape had no basis in reality, as far as I know, and yet it was a very visceral reality for me as a ten-year-old.

I started looking for references to imaginary landscapes in the literature. The library was not much help, and it came as no surprise that the card catalogue's Subject drawers contained no references to "Landscapes, Imaginary." The slide remained a mute question mark on my desk. After a long period of rummaging through different sources, I stumbled on to a curious book called *Parallel Botany* by the Italian children's book illustrator, Leo Lionni. The source of the book was the back room of a musty used bookstore in Spokane, one of those classic establishments where lots of product enters the store, but little ever leaves. Lionni had filled 200 pages with detailed descriptions of the botany of imaginary (or what he termed "parallel") plants. There were notes, appendices, quotes, references to important conferences, and illustrations, at least some of which were probably drug-induced. I was grateful to Lionni for his book, and for the support he gave to my slide of an imaginary landscape. Mr. Lionni seemed overly defensive about his parallel plants, and devoted much of his book to weaving an elaborate scientific cloak over their existence. But fortunately the beginning of each chapter contained an illustration and a natural history of such parallel marvels as woodland tweezers, strangler tirils, Cadriano germinants, and so on, as big as life:

> Uchugaki thinks that the distribution of the tweezers as we see it today is the final conquest of an intricate series of maneuvers aimed at the conquest of territory, and that these maneuvers bear the most extraordinary resemblance to the moves of the game of Go. He says that the woodland tweezers were originally sprouts from a complex rootstock that was interwoven with the roots of the *ben* tree, a huge spermatophyte which grows only in the forests of the island of Tetsugaharajima. This rootstock was like a subterranean mind, planning and storing the program for the gradual future distribution of the shoots, putting the program into action, and controlling its various phases. Strategic decisions which obeyed exact orthogenetic laws, but which simulated a fierce struggle for survival, led in the end to a kind of status quo, without winners or losers.

If plants could be imagined in such graphic detail, I thought, then certainly landscapes could be imagined too. Encouraged, I began to take walks on the mysterious landscape of my slide occasionally, throwing stones into the silver river, and touching the scrubby conifers that looked like negatives of themselves. The colors of the vegetation were those of metallic spray-paint. The botanical structures were crude, and obviously of human design.

If plants could be imagined, and then landscapes could be imagined, the next obvious step would be to create imaginary ecological successions. I believe many ordinary people would have a talent for this, since they seem to have a good intuitive grasp of actual plant succession, without actually knowing what it is. They can sense a disclimax landscape, knowing something is wrong just from the way the land looks, while knowing nothing of the climax or the process of reaching it.

To create succession on my landscape, I could plow up a swath of the barren hillside, and allow the soil to populate first with alien weeds. Then I would allow that population to collapse and follow it with successionary grasses. Probably I would insert a climax wildflower in with the grass, one whose rolled and bronze-colored leaves would act as reeds and whistle faintly in the wind. Alternatively, I could increase the rainfall over the hillside, and create a stunted forest of the negative trees.

My imaginings were not so very different from what ecologists do when they postulate real successions. We speak confidently of the oak savannah, the Douglas-fir, or the bunchgrass climax as the culmination of a determinate series of successional steps on a particular site. But none of us has ever seen any of these proposed successional sequences all the way through, from bare ground to climax. Indeed, some sequences might take 400 years or more to complete. However useful the concept of succession may be to science, it owes a very great debt to the imagination.

Landscape imagination may become useful even beyond conceptualizing successions. We need the power to imagine potential growth and verdance on the abandoned gravel pit and the tailings pile, and the thousands of landscapes we have degraded. The ability to generate parallel successions may become a key skill of the postindustrial age.

Our desire to imagine landscapes is an element of the attractiveness of certain literatures, such as travel writing, historical fiction and science fiction. We read these from a motive that is the inverse of Sir Edmund Hillary's: because the landscapes are *not* there, not visible, not with us. Our need for strangeness, and even alienness, is compelling, and the great generator of that strangeness is our own minds. The most powerful of photographs or written landscape descriptions still fall far short of the mental image that is created and retained. We viewers and readers reserve for ourselves the joys of placing, proportioning, detailing and coloring in the blanks.

The slide stayed in its viewer on my desk for a long time, and became an odd tangent to my spiral of re-exploration, a touchstone for the investigation of parallel natures. Finally, several weeks later, the actual origin of the slide suddenly occurred to me; it was the Missouri river breaks of eastern Montana. I had made a late winter driving trip from Saskatchewan to Billings to attend a scientific conference a few years before, and I had stopped briefly when I crossed the Missouri River, to stretch my legs. There was no snow, it was a clear, brutally cold day, and all the vegetation of the breaks had the bleached and windswept look of February in the northern prairies. I snapped a picture, the only one of the entire trip, and promptly forgot about it.

I labelled the location of the slide, grudgingly. The Missouri breaks were fascinating in their own right — the scrubby trees were windswept and misshapen junipers, very close to the northern limit of their range — but the actual Montana reality now seemed a bit dull alongside the parallel creation it had accidentally spawned. But perhaps I can reinvest that part of the Missouri breaks with magic, and share the posterity between myself and the landscape. As an old man, I can revisit this exact same spot, and the others I have recorded, to rephotograph it. Then I can look across thirty, forty, maybe even fifty years if I am lucky, and see a tiny slice of the magic of real succession on the landscape.

10

Tallgrass Dream

JOHN MORGAN DROPS DOWN TO HIS KNEES in the grass, and gathers a bundle of stems in his hand. His is a natural, almost unconscious movement, a tool of his profession. We are at the Living Prairie Museum, an unexpected island of native grassland in the heart of suburban Winnipeg. It is a Sunday in early spring, and several families move along the trails. I kneel down too, feeling a little self-conscious, but no one pays any attention to us, grown men kneeling in the grass.

Living Prairie is a tiny, forty-acre parcel, which the City of Winnipeg had the foresight to secure as a public ecological reserve. The vegetation we kneel in is the fabled tallgrass prairie, a grassland type whose fame and romance rivals that of the pampas of Argentina or the south African veldt. The vegetation around us is waist-high, and the growing season has not even started yet. This is a far cry from the short, droughty prairies of Saskatchewan, Alberta or Montana. At least thirty different plant species make up the complex thatch in front of us. By fall some of those plants, the statuesque grasses, will be taller than we are. It is not hard to see why Morgan, the botanist, nurseryman and prairie restorationist, takes a proprietary interest in this Living Prairie. As he methodically sorts through the plant stems in his hand, John tells me that scraps of unbroken prairie like this one are all that is left of a vast ecotype that once stretched from Chicago to Toronto, and from Lake Winnipeg to Texas. As we stand up again, I look around: a suburban neighborhood presses up on one side of us, and an industrial area looms on the other. I sense this visit will be an odyssey of loss.

I came to Winnipeg because part of my re-exploration was to meet this man who not only appreciated natural landscapes, but had the temerity and compassion to attempt to rebuild them. John Morgan approaches his work with a combination of youthful buoyancy and a kind of scientific gravity. With his ginger-colored beard, he reminds me of a young Farley Mowat, and the comparison is not inappropriate: both were trained as wildlife biologists, both spent time working in the Arctic, and both share a methodical fascination for Canadian landscapes. As with many working wildlife biologists, Morgan began his career thinking only of the animals themselves, and then gradually realized the absolute dependence of wildlife on habitat, or appropriate landscapes. Then from the habitat orientation he made an easy and graceful jump to ecosystem thinking. Put the base of the pyramid right — soil, water and vegetation — and wildlife, in all its forms, will follow.

Reserves like the Living Prairie, however damaged and imperfect they might be, are cherished points of reference for John Morgan; he tells me that of the *one million* square kilometres of the original North American tallgrass prairie, Living Prairie is part of the mere 1 per cent that still remains. Over the span of 150 years, tallgrass has disappeared like a million grains of a precious sand running down an hourglass, but this was an hourglass with no bottom. Purely by accident, a few grains of that sand are left clinging to the neck. Enter people like John Morgan and his colleague Doug Collicutt, practitioners of the new profession of ecological restoration, the healing arts as applied to landscape. They have come to know the value of those last few metaphorical grains of sand, and from that knowledge has sprung a fierce desire to protect the remaining parcels of tallgrass prairie, and to re-create others, before time literally runs out.

In its heyday, the productivity and diversity of the tallgrass was unparalleled, and its prodigious soil-building capacity left a fertile legacy that we benefit from even today. Tallgrass is to the prairie biome as rainforest is to the world's forests — the finest and most complex expression of the type. The Irish explorer Samuel Butler, who saw the tallgrass ecotype in its glory, in the 1870s, was moved to write:

> The great ocean itself does not present more infinite variety than does this prairie-ocean of which we speak. In winter, a dazzling surface of the purest snow; in early summer, a vast expanse of grass and pale pink roses; in autumn too often a wild sea of raging fire. No ocean of water in the world can vie with its gorgeous sunsets; no solitude can equal the loneliness of night-shadowed prairie....

From the small universe of his farm in nearby Argyle, Manitoba, John Morgan works to reclaim parts of our ecological patrimony, by saving and restoring tallgrass prairie. Here he catalogues the remaining scraps of Manitoba's tallgrass, produces seed and container-grown plants of tallgrass species, tests seeding methods, and undertakes actual restorations of prairie, right from the bare ground up.

The ambitious, almost quixotic profession of ecological restoration was born in the Midwestern U.S. in the late 1930s. The activities of restorationists fall into four general categories: identifying and protecting existing remnants; actually re-creating parcels of threatened ecotypes; devising management strategies for the enhancement of those existing and re-created parcels; and introducing the use of native plants into the world of home gardening and landscape architecture. The first restorationists, like Harold Green of Wisconsin, were isolated individuals, often considered either hopeless romantics, or outright heretics. A full-fledged restoration movement, with leaders and a philosophy, has emerged only recently, and the twin shadows of Thoreau and Aldo Leopold loom large over it. Morgan is part of a small group who pursue restoration full-time, but a host of others — farmers, grandmothers, schoolkids — pursue it as an avocation. In Calgary, neighborhood groups are rescuing native grassland sod about to be lost to housing developments, and transplanting it elsewhere; in Saskatoon, a university professor leads a successful citizen movement ("Rescue the Fescue") to save a small piece of relic prairie. Outside of Chicago, a conservation group uses a variety of agronomic methods to restore an abandoned farm field to the original tallgrass prairie. There is a grand irony in the fact that the original impetus for the ecological restoration movement began in the very cities that originally consumed prairie — Calgary, Chicago and Winnipeg.

The current impetus for preservation and ecological restoration seems to be the imminent threat of losing entire ecotypes. Manitoba's tallgrass certainly falls into that "threatened" category, if not beyond it: Morgan estimates the size of the province's tallgrass remnant to be $\frac{1}{20}$th of 1 per cent of its original extent.

Ecologically and geographically, tallgrass stands as a buffer between the moist deciduous forests of eastern North America and the dry plains of the West. Like the other Canadian prairie zones of mixed grass, fescue and pacific northwest bunchgrass, the tallgrass occupies a young landscape, geologically speaking. The crushing presence of the glaciers created a matrix of fine-textured soils and level terrain, and their final departure, some 12,000 years ago, left a new niche to be colonized. The ancestors of prairie plants were originally forest understory species that crept westward onto the newly-formed plains as the ice age came to a close and the glaciers departed. Tallgrass prairie, being closest to the forests, was thus the earliest type of prairie to appear on the continent. By the beginning of European settlement, the Canadian range of the tallgrass prairie covered the Red River Basin of southern Manitoba, a broad, 100-kilometre-wide swath starting at the North Dakota border and trending northeastward almost to the southern shore of Lake Winnipeg.

Tallgrass prairie species produce massive quantities of tiny, hairlike roots, an effective drought survival mechanism. Ten thousand years of this root production in the fine-textured silts and clays left by the glaciers produced some of the richest, deepest soils to be found anywhere in the world. But the prodigious soil-building ability of tallgrass prairie led to its early undoing, as the vast, fertile lands within its range were ruthlessly plowed up and planted to corn, wheat and other crops. In contrast to the drier prairies of Saskatchewan and

Alberta, where large-scale land conversion did not begin until the 1940s, Manitoba's Red River Valley was largely cultivated by the turn of the century.

Several small relict tallgrass prairies found in the Essex, Kent and Lambton counties of Ontario, separated from the Red River Basin by hundreds of kilometres of boreal forests, are a puzzle. Morgan tells me the consensus of expert opinion is that during the Altithermal, a period about 5,000 years ago when temperatures were warmer and drier than they are now, tallgrass prairie covered much of southern Ontario. As the climate cooled and forests prevailed again, a few small prairie "islands" were left. Fossil landscapes, if you will.

Like all prairies, tallgrass evolved in the presence of periodic wildfires, which, along with occasional drought, maintained a balance between grass and trees. Fire also improves nutrient cycling and prevents the buildup of excessive quantities of plant litter, which slows the normal solar warming of the soil every spring. As proof of the value of fire John cites the railroad rights-of-way, which railway workers traditionally burned as an inexpensive means of trackside vegetation control. These same rights-of-way, usually thought of as ecological disaster zones, are now some of his favorite tallgrass prairie seed collection sites, because of the vigor of the native vegetation. To be a restorationist, it seems, is to live with contradiction.

Fire was also critical to the maintenance of oak savannah, another vanished ecotype closely related to the tallgrass, which was found in the moister parts of the Red River Valley. Oak savannah consisted of widely-spaced, mature oak trees with tallgrass underneath, giving the ecotype a very pleasing, parklike appearance. Fire-resistant oak and the tallgrass species could survive the periodic fires that swept across the prairies, but fire-sensitive aspen could not. With the advent of modern fire suppression, aspen has crowded out and virtually obliterated any remaining oak savannah landscapes, and is now encroaching on many tallgrass remnants.

The early destruction of the tallgrass, and the distortion of the remnants by fire suppression, presents a real problem for Morgan; they have no blueprints upon which to model their restorations. In addition, the isolated remnants, like Living

Prairie, are always suspect, because their flora is subject to attrition from within and invasion from without. Historical descriptions of tallgrass prairie are scarce and inadequate; the early explorers hurried across it on their way to search for beaver, the Northwest Passage, or other compulsions, and few stopped to describe what they saw. The earliest recorded mention of the Canadian prairies was made in 1690 by the rhyming Irishman Henry Kelsey, who dismissed it thus:

> This plain affords nothing but beast and grass,
> and over it in three days we past.

Even Samuel Butler, who was awed by the "ocean of grass," provided lots of Victorian grandeur, but little descriptive or botanical detail to go on. I was reminded again of the importance of the nonexistent profession of landscape archeology. Much great literature has come from the simple desire to understand how things *must have been*, for a person or an era; it is time for ecologists to understand the value of this desire.

Despite the absence of historical description, Morgan and others look to a single grass, big bluestem (*Andropogon gerardii*), as a major constituent, perhaps even the backbone, of tallgrass prairie. This majestic perennial bunchgrass is the tallest of all the dryland grasses, reaching a height of two metres and curing to a rich auburn color in the fall. Switchgrass (*Panicum virgatum*) and Indian grass (*Sorghastrum nutans*) are also thought to have been present in some abundance. All three of these grasses share a complex variation of normal plant metabolism that gives them excellent growth efficiency in the heat of summer, when other plants are forced to go dormant. It is also assumed that tallgrass prairie contained a great profusion of broad-leaved plants — goldenrods, asters, blazingstars and legumes, to name a few. So the modern restorationist might envision big bluestem as the matrix of this great, buzzing, midsummer prairie enterprise. Showy, weak-stemmed goldenrods would lean against bluestem's tangled growth and shafts of purple liatris would penetrate through it. There would be white yarrow and yellow sunflowers to please the butterflies, and leadplants to taunt the botanist with their greyish, dead-looking leaves. A hundred insects, some perhaps unknown to science, could be captured in a single sweep of the net. Forgotten birds that have long since left the prairies might work the air currents above the sward, and below it the soil would teem with complex microbial life. A worthy system to restore.

People like John Morgan re-create examples of tallgrass for many reasons: as a tribute to nature, as a simple gesture atoning for our historical misdeeds to the land, or as a legacy to hand to our descendants. Or perhaps the simple feeling that an ecotype has a certain right to existence that transcends human concerns. More pragmatic reasons, like the value of biodiversity, and the maintenance of a threatened gene pool for possible future use in agriculture or medicine, may also be important. But the fundamental motive of the restorationist may be a very personal and spiritual one that is harder to define. "I can't put my finger on it," Morgan says, "but there is something very subtle and very powerful that happens when you have the privilege of kneeling quietly on a piece of tallgrass prairie."

The Morgan's farm, a quarter-section in the tiny hamlet of Argyle, north of Winnipeg in the heart of the Red River country, is where his dream and his business of tallgrass prairie restoration take shape. The cycle of restoration starts in early spring; snow has retreated to the aspen bluffs, and sheets of meltwater lie on the stubblefields. The air is full of migrating Canada geese. Doug Collicutt is a frequent visitor, as he and John discuss their plans for the coming field season. The heat has been turned on in the 1,800-square-foot greenhouse, and John and his wife Carol tend tray after tray of tiny young seedlings. Seed for these has been painfully collected from dozens of different locations: unplowed field corners, railroad rights-of-way, lightly grazed corners of cow pastures, even vacant industrial land inside of Winnipeg. The greenhouse is part production facility, part commercial enterprise (a native bedding plant business complements the Morgan's restoration consulting), and part laboratory. Here in the greenhouse's humid atmosphere the Morgans have confronted two fundamental aspects of native plant physiology: germination and root growth.

Tallgrass plant species are climax species. They are virtually all perennials, and their germinative systems are geared only to replace themselves within a very stable, long-term plant community. They are neither colonizers, like the weed species, nor highly uniform, like the crop plants. Although mature tallgrass plants can become quite large and aggressive, their seeds tend to be very small, with precise germination requirements. The seeds often germinate only after long periods of dormancy, and once they do germinate, early seedling growth can be quite slow. These long-term survival mechanisms are precisely those the plant breeder would select against when developing a crop, but the Morgans must work with these traits. They have searched the meagre literature for everything they could find on native plant germination, and have tried a full range of temperature and moisture combinations, seeding depths and seed pretreatments, in an effort to unlock the growth secrets of each tallgrass species.

Root growth of these same plants presents the opposite scenario: it is abundant, sometimes overwhelming. John laughs as he recalls their early seeding attempts using conventional two-inch-deep greenhouse cell trays. Root growth in some species was so abundant that it literally pushed plant and soil right up out of the container. John and Carol solved the problem by substituting the six-inch-deep cell trays used by silviculturists for tree seedlings.

June will find John tuning up his Ferguson tractor in preparation for seeding. In contrast to the large-scale implements his grain farming neighbors use, John seeds with a specialized, eight-foot grass drill that can deliver seed very precisely. Then he firms the soil around the seed by going over the field with a water-filled, 1,500-pound roller-packer. Morgan swears by extensive land preparation before seeding. When I suggest there is a paradox in using aggressive technology to re-create nature, he readily agrees. "No question. But right now, we use every technological trick in the book — repeated cultivation, chemical weed control, state-of-the-art seeding equipment; anything we can get our hands on that will give us good stand establishment. Otherwise, all we get is a horrendous crop of weeds."

If the planning, the land preparation, the seed, the timing, the weather and the weed control are all just right, this grueling, high-input establishment phase needs to be done only once. By the second or third growing season, the network of tallgrass perennials will have taken root and the system could, theoretically, go on forever.

Summer is a time for tending the seed nursery plots in Argyle. Classical four-by-eight research-style plots of switchgrass, stiff goldenrod, three-flowered avens, yellow coneflower and a host of other plants are laid out over two acres of sticky, gumbo soil. The Red River Basin was originally the bottom of glacial Lake Agassiz, which trapped centuries of fine, windblown silts and clays. Add to that the leaven of several millennia of tallgrass root growth, and you have a soil the color and texture of German chocolate cake. John's two young daughters, mistresses of the farmyard, wisely park their tricycles and don rubber boots before venturing into the nursery.

By crowding the nursery plants within closely-spaced rows, John has been able to induce a heavy seed set in many species. In another part of the farm, a seven-acre field has just been planted to big bluestem for seed. John and Carol have put most of their grain farming land on short-term leases, and plan to take it back as they are able to convert it to tallgrass seed production. One thirty-acre field is being prepared to be seeded to big bluestem next year. Seed harvesting of some of the early species in the nursery has begun already, and the hunt is on for good remnant harvesting sites around the countryside.

Seed harvesting begins in earnest in the fall. A pull-type harvester with a large rotary brush (similar to those seen on street sweepers) is the favored implement. This custom-made harvester, of Morgan's own design, can be set for various species by adjusting the height of the brush, the speed of its rotation and the groundspeed. John follows a strict protocol for harvesting natural areas, hitting them once only every few years, and maintaining a very broad genetic base in his seed stocks. He is also loath to send his seeds for use in distant locations, believing that the use of locally-adapted varieties is fundamental to ecological restoration. "I could easily sell my seeds to people in Calgary or Saskatoon," he says, "but that defeats the purpose of the whole exercise. The production of seed for restoration should be a local enterprise, for a local market."

After freeze-up, the farm's focus of activity shifts to the seed cleaning plant, on the second floor of a converted barn. At one end of the barn is a variety of sieves, shakers and fanning devices, all custom-made, since none of the conventional crop seed cleaning equipment works on the native seeds, which can be tiny, light, fluffy, fragile or all of the above. The rest of the barn is a motherlode of seed, stored in containers that range in size from gunnysacks to pill bottles, all neatly arranged in alphabetical order, from *Andropogon* to *Zizea*. John picks up a container at random, and shows me the tiny slivers of complexity inside. As he reseals the container, he shakes his head in bemusement. "It's funny," he says, "but I take real delight in knowing that we now have an entire ice-cream pail full of meadow blazingstar seed."

A high school playing field is an unlikely spot for a prairie restoration, but one of Morgan's most successful seedings took place at Winnipeg's Elmwood High School in 1991. Morgan and Collicutt were approached by an innovative geography teacher, Anne Monk, who was teaching a section on the Great Plains to one of her geography classes. "I am always interested in action-oriented classroom projects," she says, "and establishing a piece of tallgrass prairie seemed to combine action, learning and stewardship. It was a natural for us." The class obtained permission to rototill a little-used 2,200-square-foot chunk of the school yard. In early June, they broadcast a custom seed mix of seven grasses and twenty-five broad-leaved tallgrass species that had been collected from relic prairies. John, Doug and Anne then had the students "make like buffaloes" and press the seed into the ground. The catch was excellent, and now subsequent classes are learning to identify the true prairie species and weeding out any invaders.

Morgan and Collicutt have further honed their restoration skills in projects at Winnipeg's Kil-Cona Park and the downtown Forks redevelopment area, creating pocket prairies. They are also midway through a research project to determine the most effective means of cultivating, seeding and establishing tallgrass prairie. Some of the variables being tested are: fall versus spring seeding, drilling versus broadcasting seed, straw mulching and irrigating. They have also done some landscaping projects with prairie species, and welcome these departures from the classical tradition of mowed lawns and formal flowerbeds.

In trying to re-create prairie, Morgan is under no illusions. He is ever mindful of the ecological maxim that states "small relicts always degrade." What that means is that a five-acre prairie remnant may be forever doomed to invasion, and a five-acre restoration may never become a real, functioning prairie. Preserving or restoring tiny scraps in scattered locations may ultimately reinforce the odyssey of loss. The phenomenon of "edge effect" is one of the primary reasons; simple mathematics tells us that the smaller a parcel is, there is a greater proportion of "edge" area relative to the "inside" area, and a greater opportunity for the more aggressive introduced plants to invade from the surrounding area. This phenomenon can be seen at Living Prairie, where smooth bromegrass, a common introduced grass, can be seen invading from the adjacent land outside the reserve. Population dynamics are another problem; many species of plants and animals require a large, scattered and diverse population to maintain their gene pool. Add to this the complex and poorly understood web of interspecies dependencies, and the minimum size for a functioning, self-sufficient tallgrass prairie could easily be 500 acres, 5,000 or even more. As in the re-creation of historical fire regimes, ecological restoration work requires an awareness of our ignorance, and a good dose of humility.

Morgan himself takes a pragmatic view of what he does. "Sure, to call ourselves prairie restorationists is pretty arrogant. What we are really doing is replicating what we *think* was the original plant distribution of tallgrass prairie." He chuckles as he recalls the comment one observer made, who referred to what they were doing as "gonzo botany." "We're not even sure about the species mix, and we know there are a hundred other factors which make up a real, functioning ecosystem. But what we are doing is a start, and we are learning."

John and Carol are gracious hosts, and invite me to spend the night at their farm. Always the insomniac traveller, I was grateful that the guest bedroom was well stocked with reading material. As I read on into the still depths of this Manitoba night, I stumbled on to an essay by William Jordan of the University of Wisconsin, one of the restoration movement's theorists. As I read my interest mounted, to the point that I realized my mouth had gone dry and my palms were slightly damp. I was in the rare grip of a compelling idea that, to paraphrase Jordan, is as follows:

- Human beings have always felt a certain tension between themselves and nature.
- One of the prime functions of culture is to mediate this tension.
- Culture cannot mediate the tension between humans and nature if it operates only in the literal dimension. Successful mediation occurs when the realm of imagination, through the technologies of ritual and the performing arts, is involved.
- To the extent this is true, the real root of modern alienation from nature is not science or technology, but a loss of belief in the efficacy of ritual.
- The re-establishment of a satisfactory human bond with nature will depend on the development of the technologies of imagination and ritual.
- The process of ecological restoration provides an ideal framework for the development of a system of rituals for working out the terms of our relationship with nature.

This was grand logic: seditious, unsupported, inflammatory, but compellingly correct. Jordan doesn't ask us to back up, to some pretechnological state, nor does he ask us, as so many do, to adopt the rituals and worldviews of another culture. He asks us to go forward into our own culture, embracing both science and ritual, to devise a new paradigm for our relationship with nature. Midway through this landscape re-exploration, I knew I had sighted a major landmark.

The cycle of ecological restoration is complex and multifaceted, and Jordan sees it as a kind of reprise of human history: seed collection recapitulates hunting and gathering, as seeding does agriculture. Research activities are a capsule of science, archival work a microcosm of history. By doing restoration, we participate in and review these human advancements, their effects on us, and their effects on our landscapes. But the culmination of the restoration cycle is a humble new-old assemblage of plants, in some schoolyard, old right-of-way, or park. Restoration is a small piece of our ecological patrimony regained, a grain of sand recaptured. The attempt to actually *reproduce* an ecosystem may be an act of incredible arrogance, and yet it is also an act of profound faith in the future of nature and human beings.

I left the Morgan's farm the next day, reluctantly, and John drove me back to Winnipeg. Before going to the airport, I asked if we could stop to tour the Living Prairie once more, so I could fix that tiny shred of tallgrass landscape in my mind. As we walked the narrow footpaths, John offered an insight about his occupation. "You know, I'd like to think that the work I do is not so special or unique, that there will come a day when ecological restoration is recognized as a common profession, like medicine or law. It's good, honest work, and there's a lot of it to do." Good work. As we head back to the parking lot, I take a last look back across the prairie; lilac-tinted clouds stack up in the massive sky overhead, and the wind works its way through the tallgrass. To re-create this, or even to fail in the attempt, is certainly good work.

11

Visions of Methuselah

I WATCHED MY HAND as it passed through the water under me; a thin trail of bubbles showed its arc of motion. I was totally alone in this green and bottomless gloom. This was only a practice swim, and my wife was in a dinghy only a few feet away, but still I felt more like a shipwreck survivor than a triathlete. The skin of my hand looked almost dead white in the water. I didn't know how deep the lake was at this point, but someone had told me that not far from here an old shipwreck had been found on the bottom, *300 feet down*.

A sudden swath of colder water enveloped me, forcing my mind back to the rhythm. Concentrate, forget the shipwreck. Strokes, breathing, kicking. Nothing was going together very well. After a whole life around the water, I was beginning to realize I didn't really know how to swim. At twenty-five yards, I was unbeatable. Do thirty, sometimes forty underwater, with a special stroke my dad invented. Back flips, drifting naked down trout streams, diving off rocks, you name it, I could do it. But to actually swim, to get into a rhythm and go long distances, I could see now there was a major problem.

The morning of the race dawned clear and calm. The park next to the lake was full of people stretching, talking quietly, and jogging back and forth. Forty-four was not an ideal age for one's first triathlon, but I had my reasons for trying. I found my race number in the bike racks and began laying out my things. I had packed my backpack the night before, so everything was in the right sequence: first swimming gear, then bike shorts, then running shoes. Everyone was stretching, so I began to copy some of the moves I saw going on around me. As I did so, I recited my reasons for doing a triathlon. A milestone for the body. A challenge to my kids. A fixed event, for posterity. A physical moment broken out from the continuum of time. A spit in the devil's eye. A writer's quest for material. Pretty weird motives, all in all, but this was kind of a midpoint in my travels, and I welcomed a break from the mental intensity of the re-exploration. Whenever I return to Nelson from travels elsewhere, it reminds me of the mythical community of Brigadoon: friendly, hard to find, and slightly magic.

It seemed like the park hummed with tension, but maybe it was all my tension and no one else's. Would any one of these people around me be here for motives similar to mine? Too bad motive doesn't show, I thought, like conditioning does.

I looked down the long line of bikes, resplendent in the morning sunlight. Ethnically, they leaned heavily toward the Italian, beautiful racehorses with thoroughbred components. Disc wheels and aero bars were plentiful. I noticed that my somewhat less purebred steed was the only one with a handlebar bag and baggage racks. Hell, at six four and as much as I weigh, you don't worry about bike weight and wind resistance, I had told my teenage sons. They were demanding that either I take the bag and racks off, or else I enter the race under a phony name, to avoid family embarrassment. The handlebar bag would hold my gloves, a banana, a handtowel for sweat, and my purple sunglasses. Where would I possibly put these indispensables without a bike bag, I asked them. They had an interesting suggestion for the purple sunglasses.

Ten minutes was called and we all moved to the water's edge, like sleep-walkers. The countdown went sickeningly fast. Two minutes would go by in a heartbeat. There I was, standing waist-deep in fifty-five-degree water, in a high-speed time warp. It was then that I realized that almost everyone else had wetsuits on. The phrase "mad dogs and Englishmen" crossed my mind.

The gun was a relief, and I dived into the maelstrom of thrashing bodies.

No one had told me about the surface chop that 200 frenzied swimmers could create; my breathing rhythm, tenuous at best, was now totally thrown off. I felt like the last shark to arrive at a feeding frenzy. I switched to the old reliable, breaststroke, until the field spread out a little.

What followed was a kilometre-and-a-half of greenish and personal hell. What I had begun to suspect in those few practice swims was now coming true, in spades. The time warp experienced on the beach had now telescoped in the other direction. My reference point, a bridge pylon, seemed to be actually *receding* in the distance. Nothing worked for me except the painfully slow breaststroke. Unfamiliar goggles kept leaking. The slow current of Kootenay Lake dogged me, forcing constant course corrections. Sudden layers of frigid meltwater, straight off the Kokanee glacier, would reach out to grip my solar plexus. I was somewhere near dead last. Out of the corner of my fogged vision, I saw life-saving attendants on surfboards. They hovered, watching me with professional interest. A skin diver followed me from behind, like some predatory barracuda. This was crisis, I knew, but I was too busy fighting water demons to worry about my race time.

The brief, slimy embrace of weeds as I finally reached the beach never felt so welcome. I moved at a dazed half-jog through the transition area, to the welcome realities of terrestrial sunshine, my bike and my bag. I knew the worst was over now, and was pretty sure I could finish the race.

Prior to the triathlon I had wondered about the protocol for changing clothes. I knew lots of the serious types didn't bother, swimming, riding and running in the same gear, but there was no way I was going to bike forty-six kilometres in a wet, clammy bathing suit. So I had visions of distinctly nonathletic spectators with trench coats and Polaroids hanging around the male or female side of the transition area, depending on their preference. When it actually came down to it though, all of my wondering was pointless. I simply stripped, changed, and jumped on my bike. The compelling issue here was time, not modesty, and furthermore, the water temperature had reduced my genitals to something approaching microscopic size.

Getting on the bike was like visiting an old friend. I cranked my pedal cadence up to around ninety and headed out of town, following the sparkling lake that had been my downfall. My veteran touring bike was tuned and performing well. In bicycle terms, I figured it was about my age and condition — a well-tested workhorse, a little heavy, but with definite traces of classicism in the frame.

I passed a few people, and that boosted morale. It didn't matter that they were mainly youngsters and grandmothers. So far, the sins of the first event were not carrying over to the second. I was shifting more than ever before, mixing eighteen gears with an authority and precision I didn't know I had. Maintaining pedal cadence, over every rise and fall of the road, became an obsession. I shifted as I cornered, shifted on rough pavement, shifted as cars approached. Then I remembered the banana.

The first bite was like ambrosia. I took one more, washed it down with a little water from my bottle, and then passed another biker. I don't normally remember individual bananas I have eaten, but this one would certainly stick in my mind.

Time warped again, but this time it came to a standstill. I had started out focusing my attention on a spot on the road, about twenty feet ahead of me. Then it shifted to the front wheel, and soon I realized I was staring intently at the handlebar stem bolt. I was still pedalling at a good clip, but consciousness had quietly slipped out of gear. I shook myself, reeled in one more biker and headed back to the park. I had hoped to pass someone whose bike had high-tech disc wheels, thus vindicating grit over technology, but it was not to be.

The second transition, from bike to run, was barely notice-able. Someone whistled my bike away from me, and another took my helmet. I hoped that they were race officials of some sort. My fevered mind had already started the ten-kilometre jog while my body still struggled with the shoelaces. Okay: go back to the kindergarten rabbit-in-the-hole routine. Make a loop, go around the loop, now grasp the loose end between thumb and forefinger. My eyes bulged with concentration. The crowd stared, fascinated. Finally the knots slipped into place and I was off, liberated into yet another form of movement. Kilometre one had gone by before my legs discovered they were no longer on the bicycle.

I didn't really feel thirsty, but had a drink anyway at a water station. All the triathlete magazines I read in lieu of serious training warned of dehydration. I had no clear idea of the distance between dehydration and waterlogging, so I decided to err on the wet side.

I had to cross the big orange bridge that spanned a narrow part of the lake not far from the site of my swimming debacle. Here was yet another terror; I tried not to look down as the graceful span carried me high above the water. In addition to serious acrophobia, I had the tall man's fear of bridge railings; my fulcrum point was high enough that this railing would not stop me from falling, it would simply flip me over as I went down. I practised tunnel vision and tried to concentrate on the narrow sidewalk.

Heat began to be a factor. I had on an ancient, sleeveless T-shirt (probably the last logo-less T-shirt in existence), and it began to lengthen slowly under the burden of my sweat. At this rate, I figured it would be around my knees by about kilometre five. Thinking hard, I made a momentous tactical decision, and tucked the shirt into my shorts.

A brutal 12 per cent grade on a long, south-facing slope made me realize there were few tigers left in my tank. It was hard to stop the momentum, but I forced myself to slow to a fast walk for a minute. Before the race, I had set two personal criteria for myself: do not collapse at the finish line, and do not push yourself to the point of being a basket case for three days after the race. As I walked up the hill, I told myself I was losing time, but saving dignity.

Jogging again, I forced myself to quit listening to body talk so intently, and begin listening to the nature around me. Graceful western red cedars provided me with intermittent shade, and a tiny creek babbled and splashed as it crossed under the road. My pace steadied out, thought turned inward and then renewed, turned outward again, into the quiet and breathing and sunlit nature. Sunlight was a constant, I realized. The whole event — the run, the bike, even the swim — had been immersed in the bright amber of this cloudless August morning.

This was another view of landscape, one colored by motion, endorphins, an edge of exhaustion. The triathlon as a sporting event can potentially move us a tiny bit closer toward an earlier, more uncluttered contact with the earth. Swimming and running are natural functions, and biking is perhaps the "greenest" of our mechanical activities. Triathletes do become acutely aware of the dynamics of the beaches, backroads, mountains and oceans they compete on, and perhaps they will in time add their voices to the demand for clearer waters, cleaner air, and quieter roads.

The triathlon connects us to primordial memories of the journey and the chase, and to the even more fundamental joy of simple, unfettered movement itself. Perhaps we can push back the triathlon envelope, swimming, biking and running through nature in search of visions, like the ancient Tarahumara runners did. Postrace award ceremonies might someday disappear, along with the gaudy trophies and free shopping coupons. The replacement ceremony could recognize the spiritual parts of the athletic experience. Winners would receive not a laurel wreath, as the Greeks did, but one of western red cedar.

Kilometer eight. A slow, deliberate body rhythm had begun to fall into place. Arms swung in counterpoint to leg motion, lungs filled to capacity, and consciousness became a mildly interested third party. The only visions I could conjure up at this point were analogies with old Chevy pickups and DC-3 airplanes; absolutely reliable at slow speeds, but if you push them, the bolts and baling wire start to break. Heat dissipation became the body's prime objective, and sweat ran in great rivers. The finish line almost caught me by surprise, as I woke from a kind of endorphic trance. I gathered myself together for a presentable final sprint and then coasted into the lovely, welcoming shade of the park.

Three hours four minutes; nearly an hour off the winning pace, ten minutes more than one sixty-year-old competitor, but so be it. Now I had a baseline for the future. And I had stayed in the same race with men and women who would go on to do well in major triathlons elsewhere. Not bad. I gratefully accepted a glass of juice and sat down in the shade with my notebook. I had lots of material.

12

High Desert

THIS TIME I HEADED SOUTH AGAIN, crossing into eastern Washington and reaching the Blue Mountains of northeastern Oregon by evening. In spite of engine noise, cracked upholstery and sticking doors, the old Chevrolet van was a good travelling companion. I had a mattress in the back, my bicycle, a cooler for food, a lawn chair and even a borrowed laptop computer that would run with power from the van's battery. The first night I slept at a turnout off a secondary highway south of La Grande, rocked to sleep by John Muir's winds as they blew gently through a forest of ponderosa pine. If I were ever to become a tree hugger, ponderosa is the species that I would embrace.

The second day I continued southward through the Blues, again on secondary highways. I was going to California to visit my father, but not by any particular direction. The mountains were deeply incised by occasional river valleys, and every hour or so I crossed another low pass. It was slow going, but I was reassured to see this much natural space, to know that amidst all the hyperdevelopment of the Western Interior, there were still places you could drive for an hour and not see anyone, places that would continue unchanged beyond your own mortality.

Somewhere around Burns, I crossed a physiographic

boundary, leaving the Columbia Plateau and entering Great Basin country. If ponderosa pine were to symbolize the plateau, then sagebrush would represent the basin, a vast shallow bowl of semidesert and desert, over which lies the state of Nevada, plus parts of Utah, California, Arizona and New Mexico, as well as this part of Oregon. The Great Basin is hydrologically closed: the little water that falls within it stays within it, and while doing so, it washes the earth's soluble minerals slowly, inexorably to the very bottom of the basin, the great Salt Lake. This physiographic boundary between plateau and basin is far more important to the life of the landscape than any political boundary.

I spent the next night on the grounds of an isolated research station at the foot of Squaw Butte, a place name of some current embarrassment, in east-central Oregon. As is my habit, I wanted to learn a bit of the mechanics of a landscape before releasing myself to be alone with it, so the next morning I visited with one of the station's scientists, Rick Miller. Rick showed me the structure of the area's high desert vegetation, which is composed mainly of Wyoming big sagebrush, stipa grass, and Idaho fescue. He also showed me the small juniper trees that were gradually colonizing hillsides and draws, any areas where there was the least bit of northern exposure. It was a familiar story: fire-sensitive juniper, traditionally a minor part of the area's flora, had increased dramatically over the five or six decades since fire suppression had become effective.

I thanked Rick for his time and went on to climb Squaw Butte, a symmetrical cone that rose several hundred feet above the land surface. This was the high desert, a great plain at 4,000 feet that receives only eleven inches of precipitation, virtually none of it in the summer. I stopped frequently to examine the tortured outcrops of lava rock. It wasn't long before I spotted a tiny horned lizard, skittering over rocks that were the color of clotted blood.

From the top of the butte and to the east I could see Steens Mountain, another prominence rising above the desert. To the west, I could just make out the first foothills of the Cascades. Other than the research station, the gravel access road, and a fading jet contrail, no other signs of human activity could be seen in a complete full-circle sweep. The scenery did not meet the conventional canons of western landscape majesty — no spectacular mountains, no crashing waterfalls or exotic cacti, but it was profoundly, achingly beautiful. And I had the privilege of being in it, of being off the road, off the page, and in the landscape itself. The deep well began to flow again.

I stayed rooted for a long time on the exposed lava rock at the top of the Butte, recalling Rick's comment that it was a place "where you don't have to erase the word solitude from the dictionary." Could much of the wilderness experience we crave actually be the increasingly rare encounter with solitude, in the sense of seeing neither humans nor direct evidence of their works?

As I sat, the colors of the butte, of grass, sagebrush and rock, of sky and cloud, seemed to poise on an increasingly narrow balance point of perceived reality, and seemed ready to tip at any second into a transformed dimension. The mild fabric of air, tethered between Steens Mountain and the Cascades, tugged at me gently. I felt my persona becoming slightly unstable, with no gyproc walls and urban disturbance there to hold it together. It was as if my consciousness might break up in a silent explosion of borders, and individual fragments would fly out to merge with different parts of the landscape — to the soft grey of Wyoming big sage, the blood red of fissured lava rock, the proud yellow columns of Idaho fescue.

I pulled back, wondering if these feelings were like those of an epileptic or mental patient, just before an uncontrolled state comes on. Then I felt suddenly self-conscious, sitting for no reason on a cinder cone in the Oregon High Desert. It was the old embarrassment, the same one that I had felt on the Kokanee Ridge. Spirituality has always seemed risky in practical situations, and there was half a lifetime of practical behind me. I dismissed the embarrassment as a luxury that, in middle age, I could no longer afford.

It is costly, in personal terms, to go from the practical to the mystical. As Leonard Cohen says:

> I came so far for beauty
> I left so much behind

> My patience and my family
> My masterpiece unsigned

We have acculturated ourselves not to deal with the spiritual. Religion is couched in dogma and not open to forging personal, heretical links with landscape. We don't even have adequate language to make the attempt (try to define *spiritual, mystical, transcendent* without getting lost in abstraction and qualifying statements). Everyone's experience of the spiritual is by definition unique, making it even more difficult to explain. And yet I feel an urgency to go in, to open the door and enter this personal room I have imagined, shaped, and created, but have barely seen.

In our society, there is an almost automatic reference to aboriginal or Far Eastern cultures whenever nature or land-based mysticism is considered. There is no question that these cultures are far ahead of ours when it comes to spiritual connections to the landscape, but for us to concentrate so exclusively on foreign approaches amounts to an elaborate cop-out. By borrowing other peoples' rituals and approaches, which have little or no chance of serious, mainstream adoption, we neatly avoid the central question of building a spiritual connection to the land into our own culture. This is cultural appropriation of the worst kind.

The vague spiritual component of my own re-exploration was slowly becoming clearer to me. Honky agnostic land-based mysticism, I called it. Passion is not used to so many qualifiers. I must search through every nook and cranny of my own culture, and stitch together any pathetic scraps of land-based spirituality I can find. And if I can't find enough, I could become the honky spirit warrior, grease myself down, and run until I generate the Celtic visions, and find the revelations on the cusp between nature's chaos and nature's order.

I left the butte and the research station by a different road, actually more a track than a road, that wound through the gently undulating sage-covered landscape. Half an hour out, and still nowhere near the highway, the van engine began to lose power and cough. My mind and pulse began to race as I nursed it along. Should I go back to the station, or try to get out to the highway? This was indeed a lonesome part of the world. My bicycle was in the back, a kind of life-raft I could use to go and get help if I had to. By now I was just creeping along, barely keeping the engine alive. Finally I pulled over, shut the engine off and walked out into the sage to contemplate my options. Suddenly the landscape didn't look nearly as spiritual. I looked back balefully at the transformed van, now a traitor instead of a trusted travelling companion. I walked some more, getting hold of my anxiety. I had not given my dad a precise arrival time, so an extra day or even two wouldn't matter. I could probably get help, and knowledge of older automotive engines is endemic in rural areas like this. Maybe I could even find the problem and fix it myself. I went back to the van and popped the hood. In five minutes, I had found and reconnected a vacuum hose that had come loose from the carburetor, and got the engine running properly again. The sagebrush seemed a little friendlier.

As I pulled back on to the track, I realized there was a rich irony here; all morning I had been on intimate and spiritual terms with the environment, and now a loose vacuum hose caused that mode to suddenly evaporate. Nature had become an antagonist, to be challenged in some primitive way and overcome. The sagebrush, which together with the antelope and horned toad can trigger in me such feelings of intimacy and passionate interest, care not a fig for me. They are all committed to a single purpose even more primitive than survival: the passing on of their DNA. And here I am imposing my flights of fancy and temporary epiphanies on their uncaring genes. The antithesis of love is not hatred, it is indifference.

The nonliving part of nature is even less responsive than the biotic part: if we define purpose in human terms, the ever-changing earth and sky have none at all, and don't give a damn whether I live or die. Our approach to nature is such a curious box of sacredness, fear, curiosity and resource exploitation.

Finally I reached Highway 395, a desolate ribbon of two-lane blacktop, and turned south again. The Albert Rim, a massive escarpment near Lakeview, reminded me again of my unfulfilled wish to learn the logic of geology. I spent that night in Alturas, a small town just across the border in California. The next morning I walked around for a while, and then phoned my dad, to tell him I was in a pleasant little town called Alturas, and that I would arrive sometime that evening. Dad caught me by surprise when he told me we had been to Alturas once, when I was a small child, and that I seemed to like it then, too. I had absolutely no recollection of the town or the area: it was at that point that I realized that landscape nostalgia can root in the unconscious as well as in the conscious mind.

From Alturas I angled southwest, through the mixed pine forests of the Mount Lassen country. I have a fascination for ecotones, and I knew I was on one when I saw the first oak appear, a herald of the open, Mediterranean-style grasslands of the Coast Range, where my father lived.

Not long after this planned trip came another, unplanned one, a huge and unresolved kink in the spiral of re-exploration, when my father died. He was the one who first introduced me to the landscapes of the Western Interior, and let me swim every river from the Sacramento to the Quillayute. Our relationship had run a fifty-year gamut of hunting chukar in sagebrush, to vicious arguments about the nature of patriotism and finally to a relaxed acquiescence and mutual love of old books. He and I had always been solitary satellites, in distant communication, whose orbits drifted close occasionally. Now I would be tumbling on alone.

The lonely midwinter trip to California, the one to pay last respects, was more hurried than the last one, so I took Highway 97, which angles southward from the Canadian border to Weed. It was a good highway to think on, and one volcanic peak or another was almost always in view. As I travelled between Klamath Falls and Weed, around the massive flanks of Mount Shasta, I realized that a memorial for my father was redundant. It already existed, right here, in this stretch of country he knew so well. Natural landscapes are fountains of spirituality, but they can also offer great comfort.

13

Mediterranean

My SISTER'S HOUSE straddles a narrow ridge, the kind that suburban San Franciscans love to build on. Just beyond her backyard is a massive, curving hillside, spared from development by its steep, almost giddy slope. I could see from her window that this hillside was dotted with pampas grass, tick brush, and occasional eucalyptus groves.

As we visited for several days, sharing the pleasure of piecing together a common mosaic of our childhood, the hillside stayed in the background. The landscape kept reminding itself to me though, and early one morning, before anyone was up, I simply bolted out the back door and over the fence. Neighborhood dogs were outraged. I half-skied down the slick bunchgrasses that anchored the steep slope. Partway down the hill, I came across a children's path that looped elegantly across the concave surface, and I followed it for a way.

There was plenty of lizard habitat here, old slabs of plywood and rotting boards. To this day I have trouble passing a rotted log or board without stopping to turn it over, a childhood habit that started on these same California hillsides.

I finally stopped at a likely-looking old board and lifted it up slowly. Sure enough, nestled in a depression in the earth, was a resplendent alligator lizard, about ten inches long. A rush of pleasant memories made me pause, and the lizard was semidormant in the December weather, so we just sat and eyed each other for a long time. Whether I wanted to admit it or not, I was definitely in the midst of a re-exploration of the landscapes of my childhood.

Alligator lizards are smooth-skinned and snakelike, with powerful jaws for crushing grasshoppers, young mice, and whatever else comes along. By some evolutionary fluke, their jawline is fixed into a kind of happy-go-lucky grin, and their yellow eyes glitter, so they have the look of amiable bandits. These lizards also have a long prehensile tail that they will detach immediately if you grab them with anything less than total finesse. This is a brilliant defence mechanism: because of the lizard's alertness and speed, if the predator (be it snake, cat or small boy) catches it at all, it will nearly always catch it by the tail, which promptly detaches and writhes about, creating a momentary distraction while the rest of the lizard escapes. It then grows a new tail, and gets the last laugh, which may explain the grin. These animals were a joy for me to keep as childhood pets, because they are active and eat almost everything.

This lizard, *Gerrhontus*, is very cosmopolitan. It ranges into Mexico and north to the Okanagan and the Kootenay valleys of southern British Columbia. On a recent trip to B.C.'s Gulf Islands, I spotted one on a dry, south-facing hillside. Not surprisingly, that hillside too was very mediterranean, clothed in annual grasses, oaks, and what Canadians call arbutus and Americans call madrona.

I laid the board back down gently over the dormant lizard, and wandered farther downhill to a grove of huge eucalyptus trees. I knew my sister would understand my absence, since she too had participated in childhood rambles over hillsides like this one.

The inside of the grove was like an airy and quiet cathedral. Eucalyptus, the "gum" tree of Australia, is an immigrant that has completely naturalized itself in large parts of California. The ground was a bit more level here, and I became absorbed by the great naked trunks and their peeling, stringy bark. Filtered shafts of light slanted down through the canopy and the air was heavy with the dry, camphorated smell of eucalyptus oil. This was botany as religious architecture, I was thinking, when suddenly, belatedly, a discordant shape jarred me back to alertness. There was a man, somewhat younger than I, sitting motionless with his back against a eucalyptus. He wore wire-frame glasses and a red baseball cap, and a greasy, worn pack lay by his side. I had the sensation of suddenly seeing a wild animal and realizing that it had been studying me for some time.

This was an impasse. I felt an urge to prattle on excitedly about this intersection of ecology and memory, to share my pleasure with this person who could be a version of myself. At the same time, my head blazed with thoughts of California crime rates, expensive drug dependencies, psychopathic alienation, and my family back home. We had interrupted one another's reveries. Mine was bemused-botanical, but I had no idea of the nature of his. In the end, I said something totally inane like "howdy" and walked on. He said nothing.

The hillside was like an open book for me, the man in the baseball cap an enigma. Few people would choose such a spot to inhabit, even for a few moments, but he and I both did. Had I remained a Californian, we might have been blood brothers, or perhaps one another's victim. I knew an actual exchange between us would have been significant, in some way.

I returned to my sister's house with one perfect memory of an alligator lizard, and one small, lasting regret.

14

The Nature of Natural

A CONFERENCE BROUGHT ME to the southern Alberta town of Lethbridge, by way of the Crowsnest Pass and then gliding down the Eastern Slopes of the Rockies. A veteran of these three-day environmental and biological get-togethers, it is my custom to make brief escapes from them, to carry some of the ideas from the conference presentations out into the actual landscape itself, to see how they play. By the second afternoon of this event, after a lengthy discussion of ecosystem management, I was ready to make my escape.

I changed into running shoes and sweats and headed off the university campus, into Lethbridge suburbia. The wide spaghetti streets of the new subdivision stretched out over land that was recently wheatfields and before that, prairie. The houses and streets were totally empty. I felt like I was jogging through a neighborhood that had suffered some kind of futuristic smart-bomb holocaust: everything neatly in place, right down to the tricycles on the lawn, the wheeled plastic garbage cans neatly parked at the curb, the planted Siberian elms, but no people. Not a soul.

The spaghetti roads finally ended near the edge of the Oldman River valley, the destination I had chosen for my escape. To get from the edge of the suburb to the valley I had to cross a summerfallow field. I could feel the plowed soil slowly accumulating in the treads of my running shoes; I guessed it was a clay loam. It struck me that in the mountains of my home, I would divide up the landscape by river drainage, but here on the prairies, I would use soil type. Mountain, prairie, Canadian, American. These are the difference engines that drive my consciousness as a traveller, and re-explorer.

Looking back, the field seemed slightly pathetic. It was probably tied up in real estate litigation, as it patiently awaited its final conversion to suburbia. At the farther edge of the summerfallow was a small side coulee that led down into the main valley. In contrast to the tidy suburb, garbage lay everywhere here. Shrubs were festooned with plastic shopping bags that fluttered in the constant southern Alberta wind. The piles of rotting tarpaper and gyproc had no doubt originated from the neat suburb behind me. An official-looking sign said "Community Space, No Dumping." It should more properly have read "The Tragedy of the Commons."

I see that the native prairie in the coulee has largely been hijacked by the alien bromegrass, cheatgrass and crested wheatgrass. Dirt bike and ATV tracks scar the sides of this dry valley. Yet in spite of the devastation, I have to acknowledge remnants of the natural that begin to appear as I descend the side coulee. First a clump of buckbrush, then a Saskatoon, and farther on a patch of the shy muhly grass. Rounding a steep headland into the main valley, I see bare layered earth and stone — erosion that oddly enough, amongst all this disturbance, is probably natural. In the space of fifteen minutes, I had travelled from the spaghetti roads of Marlborough Place to uncovered layers of the Miocene past.

My purpose in this pastoral escape is to road test the conference discussions on ecosystem management. Managing environment and natural resources with reference to how they functioned in an undisturbed, "natural" state is one definition of ecosystem management, although there are others. Given my surroundings, it is hard to contemplate that definition without some irony. What about the exposed soil of these dirt bike tracks? What is *their* historical precedent? The bare ground they create is an ecological insult, the zero point of succession.

It would take a hundred years to rebuild an inch of this valley's lost topsoil. Again I temper my anger by reminding myself that some of the bare ground here is from natural slumping of these steep, young valley sides. Could ecosystem management define a sustainable level of soil disturbance, and a ratio between natural versus anthropogenic disturbance?

What about the invading grasses that clog the hillsides around me? How would I put them into an ecosystem management framework? Could I somehow determine a natural, pre-European contact rate of new species invasion, and then make sure that the arrival of these alien bromes and fescues and agropyrons does not exceed that rate?

I reach the main valley and turn to follow the Oldman upstream. The mature cottonwoods in the riverbottom are dying and no new seedlings are visible, probably because a new dam upriver has disrupted the spring flooding process that is vital to cottonwood regeneration. This whole valley is a kind of celebration of disturbance and contempt, capped by the railroad bridge that spans it from rim to rim. The High Level Bridge is like the Eiffel Tower laid down, a massive black iron structure 300 feet high and a mile long. It is an overwhelming and iconic denial of this valley, this rare contour in the flat prairie landscape. Built by the Canadian Pacific Railroad in 1909, the High Level has seen seven deaths, only two during construction, but five more to subsequent suicides. I could visualize the high iron fretworks producing an eerie music when the winds were just right.

I am busy cultivating a kind of ecological disgust as I approach the weathered concrete pylons that support the railway bridge, when something brings me up short. There, in a barren pile of overburden, right at the very foot of one of humanity's larger structures, is a thriving patch of the delicate and fussy native blue grama grass.

I stop for a closer look, my body welcoming the suggestion to stop running. The spoil pile is a coarse and yellowish gravel, the raw and inhospitable excreta of glaciers. Yet the blue grama is spreading nicely on it, and has produced large numbers of the curled, one-sided seedheads that always remind me of fuzzy caterpillars. It is a horrendous site for any plant, let alone a climax grass. The blue grama must have negotiated a very, very careful trade, I reasoned, accepting the multiple hostilities of the spoil-pile site in exchange for the lack of competition from other plants. No matter how I worked out the dynamics of the site, though, the grass's presence was still an anomaly in my ordered, ecological universe. The shock of pristine nature encroaching on gross human disturbance is as disturbing as encroachments of the opposite kind.

Resuming my run down the trail, I decide this blue grama and I share a common characteristic: we are both out of place. My instincts are ecological but I am rooted in the real-world spoil pile of natural resource management. That means I am condemned to a particular form of purgatory in my professional life: of wearing a cowboy boot on one foot and a Birkenstock sandal on the other. While not a full participant in the views and lifestyles of either the redneck or the environmentalist camp, I am drawn to the ecology of nature at the same time I am drawn to the ways of using natural resources, particularly those on public land. This is why ecosystem management so intrigues me: it may provide a workable, overarching theory for those like myself who are inoculated with barbed wire and boot caulks, but who still see wisdom in the landscape.

Ecosystem management — a total re-exploration of the field of natural resource management — is based on first determining the ecological "limits," the highs and lows, of landscapes and organisms as they functioned in a natural state, undisturbed by humans. Once those limits are determined, then we can shift the management of those landscapes and organisms toward maximum economic and social benefit, so long as we stay within the limits. The theory is based on the assumption of a certain rate of natural disturbance, and natural change; that landslides, climatic fluctuations and grasshopper outbreaks have always occurred and will continue to occur, and that we are able to keep our own disturbances similar in scale, quality and frequency to the natural ones. Ecosystem management is a progressive and compelling new concept for the use of natural resources, certainly a step beyond the previous paradigm, which Gifford Pinchot articulated as "the greatest good for the greatest number." Democratic it was, but sustainable it was not.

The very term "ecosystem management" sounds arrogant: forests and valleys and rivers can manage themselves, thank you very much, and have done so for many thousands of years. The phrase should be understood to mean "the manipulation of a natural ecosystem for human benefit, by using and mimicking natural processes, while staying within that ecosystem's range of historical variability." The theory will only work if we first commit to the historical and contemporary investigation required to establish the goalposts and processes, and then further to bind our society to staying within those goalposts.

I try to visualize this Oldman valley in ecosystem management terms. Certainly the High Level Bridge is far outside the bounds of natural, but it probably doesn't really impair the natural processes of the valley, and it is certainly a haven for pigeons. I need to look beyond the symbolic impact of these structures to their functional importance. The four-lane Trans-Canada Highway that crosses the valley a few kilometres distant is likely a more serious disturbance, stopping terrestrial movement of any number of species. Could ecosystem management allow me to set ecological limits for the disruption of natural movement corridors?

I lope farther along the valley's trails, enjoying a taste of what pleasure the coyote feels, but still two-footedly mindful of protruding rocks and cottonwood roots. As I pass another side coulee, I notice the upper portion of it has been burned. My guess is the architects of the burn were probably skulking adolescents who, in their own heedless way, replicated the natural process. So here was another road test for ecosystem management: fire.

Historically fire-maintained dry forests, like those of Alberta's Eastern Slopes, now just hidden by the valley rim, are perhaps the central paradox of ecosystem management. In the case of the dry pine, fir and larch forests of the North American West, it is possible to develop stand histories and fire chronologies from say, 1650 to 1850, admittedly a minute slice of ecological time, but one that would show modern fire regimes in an essentially natural state. The fire chronology is used not strictly to provide an *average* fire return rate, but to determine the *extremes*; what was the longest interval without fire, and what was the shortest. With ecosystem management, we don't necessarily want to *replicate* the precontact forest stand architecture and fire regime (although that may be a valid goal in certain wilderness areas), rather we want to keep the stand *within the range of its historical variability,* to borrow Charles Kay's phrase. So long as we stay within those goalposts, we can manage the forest for the best mix of selfish economic and social benefits.

No wonder I am attracted to ecosystem management: it requires an understanding of changes to the landscape over time, and a grasp of the elaborate minuet of succession and disturbance. It provides a motive for re-exploration, another solution for the intractable problem of nostalgia, and a use for all those slides I have taken.

The modern understanding of fire-maintained ecosystems is poised to throw another paradox at us: Stephen Pyne, Charles Kay and others have done extensive studies of the sources of fire ignition in these ecosystems prior to European contact, and have concluded that while some fires were started by lightning, the majority appear to have been started by humans. This throws our whole concept of "natural" into complete question. If aboriginals habitually burned certain landscapes over hundreds of years, then is that the "natural" historical situation? If we decide it is, then what if an aboriginal person starts a fire now? What if a Caucasian starts a fire now? If we are trying to preserve one of these landscapes in a "natural" wilderness or park state, then are we duty-bound to start fires in it?

The traditionally firm natural ground suddenly goes very swampy.

If one side of the ecosystem management coin is the mimicking of natural processes within the range of historical variability, then the other side is the even greater conundrum of the preservation of natural disturbance. Forest fires in national parks, brucellosis outbreaks in wild ungulate populations, mudslides in pristine watersheds — if it can be truly determined that these events do occur in the absence of human intervention (a determination that is becoming more difficult every day) then they should be allowed to occur, where possible. In Loren Eiseley's essay, "The Star Thrower," Eiseley meets an enigmatic figure walking a Mexican beach after a storm. Starfish have been thrown up on the beach by the power of the storm-tossed surf, and the star thrower is hurling them back in to the sea, so they may survive. This act, which Eiseley seizes upon as profoundly altruistic, is, in a certain way, also profoundly wrong-headed. The death of starfish as a result of Mexican coastal storms is an absolutely natural process, a legitimate part of the whole phantasmagorical enterprise of nature, and those deaths should be allowed to proceed. Exceptions may be made, however, for the production of great essays.

Natural extinctions are another conundrum. Most biologists are willing to recognize that North America would have lost certain plant and animal species even if Europeans had never colonized it. Separating natural extinctions from human-induced extinctions demands the judgment of ten-thousand-year processes with the very limited experience of about 300.

How we define ecosystem management is very dependent on our view of the relationship of the human to nature. Earlier in the conference, I had been able to survey the delegates on this relationship, by asking the question, "Do you consider yourself part of nature, or separate from it?"

I myself waffle on this one, so I anticipated a response that was fairly evenly divided, something like half-and-half. The result in fact was overwhelmingly one-sided: close to 90 per cent of this group of biologists, academics and land managers considered themselves to be a part of nature. One's answer to this question, I belatedly realized, carries a great deal of ethical cargo with it. If we see ourselves as part of the continuum of nature — as a kind of very specialized animal — then we have the basis for a kinship with other animals, plants, and ultimately the Earth itself. On the other hand, calling ourselves part of nature can also offer a rationale for *all* our actions, no matter how destructive. If I drain a marsh to put in a shopping mall, or spill heavy oil in the ocean, I am simply acting out my role as a human animal, a part of nature, so therefore my actions are justified, understandable, and forgivable by that same nature.

Even the very progressive ecosystem management schemes being put in place by federal agencies in the U.S. Pacific Northwest specifically include human social and economic needs as part of their definition of an "ecosystem."

To see oneself as an extension of nature does not guarantee a sustainability ethic. The Indian subcontinent is home to human cultures that are profoundly animistic and reverential to nature, yet parts of that region have experienced massive anthropogenic deforestation and overgrazing to the point that topsoil has been totally eliminated. The current theories about the demise of the Easter Island human culture are rooted in overcutting and the destruction of the island's forests, in an ominous foreshadowing of Dr. Seuss's book, *The Lorax*. The Easter Island scenario seems particularly graphic, because it operated in the closed system of a small group of islands, but North America today is rapidly approaching closed-system status, since we can now project the endpoints of many of our resources. All human cultures, whether they are primitive, nature-reverent, or technological, seem to have the capacity to destroy the environment that sustains them.

The opposite theory, of placing the human outside of and separate from nature, has some compelling evidence to support it. We humans have the unique blessing and curse of self-awareness. We lever ourselves and nature through technology. We seem to have no instinctive checks on population size and carrying capacity. We foul our own habitat, and we kill our own kind on a regular basis. All characteristics that are certainly grounds for expulsion from the club of nature.

Seeing ourselves as separate from nature could lead to a kind of Old Testament arrogance where we see nature as subjugate to our needs. Placing ourselves outside of nature could also generate an increase in our already pervasive sense of alienation and isolation. Being the only human beings in our solar system and probably in our galaxy, it is not a comforting thought to cut ourselves off from nature as well. The positive side, though, is that a sense of apartness could provide us with the opportunity to grant nature independent standing, to recognize it as a spontaneous entity separate from ourselves, with potentially infinite complexity and rights to its own existence. I like the concept that nature can never be totally contained within our cosmologies and understandings — it is important for me personally that a part of nature remain forever unknowable. For us to define this separation from nature may make it easier to finally acknowledge and confront our own bent toward destruction and self-destruction, since we would no longer have the false cover of "animal instinct" and "natural behavior" to rely on.

Whether we see ourselves as part of or separate from it, either theory can be manipulated to denigrate nature; likewise either theory carries with it the potential for a respectful view.

The expanse of bottomland I was running on narrowed and finally disappeared. The gentle trail had now become a narrow, side-hill deer scramble, so I turned around. Retracing my steps, I passed by the burn, under the High Level Bridge, around the disturbing spoil pile, and finally to the side coulee that took me back up into suburbia. I reminded myself that I had been part of the very birth of this suburban phenomenon — of tracts of houses dropped onto timeless yellow grass — as a kid in 1950s southern California. When the fields I used to explore changed almost overnight to dozens of nearly identical houses, which often sat empty for long periods, I would, in typical omnivorous boyhood way, shift to exploring the insides of those houses. Each house had a brand new automatic washing machine, and inside each washing machine, in screaming orange-yellow complementary splendor, sat a large economy-size box of Tide detergent, which our new televisions told us got clothes whiter than white.

Fortunately, it was after five o'clock now, the effects of the smart bomb had worn off, and Lethbridge's suburbia was coming back to life. People were about, the tricycles were being ridden, and garbage cans were being wheeled back into two-car garages. I felt out of place here, too, running slowly along the spaghetti streets, but no matter. Like the blue grama on the spoil pile, I would make my exchanges, and carry on.

⊙

15

On Suspect Terrain

IN JOHN HUSTON'S *The Treasure of the Sierra Madre*, three unemployed drifters meet in Tampico and decide to go prospecting for gold. Life improves for the three once they leave the city. After a long journey through the desert, the men find wealth and destiny at a remote claim in the Sierra Madres. Howard (played by Walter Huston), the grizzled old philosopher of the trio, insists that the mine site be restored before they leave it, as a way of showing their gratitude to the Earth for giving up its fortune to them. On the return trip through the desert, the greed and paranoia of Dobbs (Humphrey Bogart) are the trio's undoing. The climactic scene, where Dobbs shoots Curtin and leaves him for dead, is filmed within a nightmarish tangle of black, leafless tree branches. Dobbs goes on alone, but he is waylaid and killed by bandits. The bandits mistake the bags of gold for sand, and dump them out. Desert winds soon blow the gold dust and the bags away, but one empty bag catches on a prickly pear cactus. Meanwhile, Curtin recovers; he and old Howard pick up Dobbs' and the bandits' tracks and follow them through the desert. Finding the empty bag on the cactus makes them realize their fortune is gone, a realization that precipitates one of the more Olympian laugh scenes in cinematic history.

I am a student of film as well as of landscape, although

there is no obvious connection between the two. Perhaps it is because I have always wanted to find a connection between my two parallel fascinations that I conceived of an experiment, a test of the relationship between nature and the movies. Seeing the *Treasure of the Sierra Madre* convinced me that there was at least a possibility for moving landscape to center stage in a film.

My interest in movies had a rather idiosyncratic origin. When I worked in rural Colombia, I had a friend and colleague named Richard, who was a serious film student and auto-didact. On weekends, he would drag me along to the big city to watch movies. This meant taking tortuous twelve-hour bus rides, surviving mudslides, engine fires and military check-points, in order to get to Bogota for two days of movies. When we arrived at the bus station, I would lay in food, beer and supplies while Richard pored over the entertainment page of *El Espectador*, arranging the day's itinerary. Since the first features started at two o'clock in the afternoon, we could see three, sometimes four movies in a day, shuttling between theatres. Fortunately, the movies were very cheap and a good mix of American, European, and Mexican releases was available. After two grueling days, we would get back on the bus, and Richard would patiently explain the failings, dramatic reaches, cinematic references and symbolic overtones of the films we had seen, and the twelve-hour bus trip would go by in a flash.

The residue of those trips with Richard was a permanent interest in movies, and the separate interest in nature compelled me to watch closely any film that made use of natural landscapes. I got in the habit of staying on through to the credits, not to see who the actors were, but to catch the fine print at the very end of the reel that told where the movie was filmed. As the stock of movies I had seen slowly increased, I began to puzzle over why so few of them made good use of natural landscape. The sister media of painting, still photography and classical music are virtually obsessed with natural landscape, yet the medium of film ignores it.

The experiment would be part of my re-exploration. Being a gentleman scientist, and aware of my own tendencies toward advocacy, I went as far as posing a null hypothesis; there are no feature films, other than documentaries, that actually use natural landscapes as part of the dramatic action of the plot. In other words, the landscape must be used for more than just a backdrop for the movie's action in order for it to score a hit in my experiment. In true scientific fashion, I set about trying to prove the null hypothesis wrong. I purchased a VCR and got a membership card at Reo's, a local independent video store, and watched a virtual orgy of movies, starting with the *Treasure of the Sierra Madre*. With three or four a night, it was like Bogota all over again, but I missed Richard.

As I collected my data, I soon found that the films I was seeing began to fall into the separate categories of desert, jungle, prairie, arctic, mountain, coastal, and river. Of the "desert films," I think *The Treasure of the Sierra Madre* is perhaps the outstanding example. *Lawrence of Arabia, Melvin and Howard, PowWow Highway* and *Thelma and Louise* also have desert settings that figure significantly in their plots. Desert seems to prompt feelings of freedom, and escape from inhibitions, in the characters of these films. In *Thelma and Louise*, the progression from the Route 66 trucker culture westward through the agricultural belt and finally to wide open desert is paired with the two protagonists' increasing clarity about their personal situations. By the time they reach the desert, they are outside the cultural envelope, so to speak. Desert has also been used as a metaphor for emotional blankness (*Paris, Texas;, Zabriskie Point*). One should be careful about interpreting the cinematic use of desert too profoundly; it may have purely accidental cachet simply because it is the natural landscape closest to Hollywood.

Jungle films are a contrast. It would be tempting to suggest that film-makers always use jungle settings to convey claustrophobia (as in *The Piano*) or moral corruption (*At Play in the Fields of the Lord; Emerald Forest*). But two notable jungle films — *The Mission* and *Fitzcarraldo* — portray the opposite emotion of liberation.

In the course of my experiment, I realized that one's view of the movies is necessarily imperfect, due to availability and predilection. For example, I have been trying to see another jungle film, *Aguirre, the Wrath of God*, for at least ten years, without success. Other films that are available and come highly recommended I simply won't see, out of sheer perversity. Still others may contain good use of landscape but feature an actor or actress that I simply don't like. Powerful individual scenes in mundane films can also complicate matters. The first five minutes of *Far From the Madding Crowd*, for instance, when Alan Bates's sheepdog comes unhinged and drives a herd of sheep at dawn across the moors and over a cliff, is riveting. The rest of the movie definitely isn't. The opening scene of *The Keep*, where the camera pans slowly and relentlessly down a distant, forested hillside, then to the rearview mirror of a moving army truck, in which we see Jurgen Prochnow's face in the flare of a sulphur match as he lights a cigarette, is a magnificent introduction to the eerie landscape of a very ordinary movie. My own quirkiness in appreciating film leads me to believe that film criticism has potential for the same cranky idiosyncrasy that marks literary criticism.

Films I found to have significant prairie or grassland plots are *Dances with Wolves, Out of Africa, Heartland, A Perfect World*, and *Badlands*. The last scenes of *Dances with Wolves* are set in a forest landscape, but it is a very special forest — the Black Hills of North Dakota, which is surrounded by, and spiritually belongs to, the prairie. This film also hints at the theme of ecological restoration as Kevin Costner endeavors to clean up the abandoned army camp he occupies.

Never Cry Wolf, Salmonberries and *Map of the Human Heart* are three good arctic films, although they tend to hurry through their landscapes to get on with the human interactions. In *Never Cry Wolf*, when the bush pilot abruptly leaves tenderfoot Farley Mowat (Charlie Martin Smith) and all his gear in the middle of a frozen lake, what follows is a classic evocation of the awe, fear and desolation that an arctic landscape can inspire.

Rivers are not very well served by movies, other than in *A River Runs Through It*. The 1962 short film *The Occurrence at Owl Creek Bridge* contains outstanding river images that are central to the plot, but it is almost completely unavailable. Director Ingmar Bergman has a lock on coastlines as a landscape, in films like *The Seventh Seal*. It has been pointed out that the beach as a natural landscape in American film has been totally hijacked by cultural concerns, starting with *Beach Blanket Bingo*. In other words, there is "massive mediation" of our view of beach nature by the media concerns of the day.

There are no good mountain or forest films, I have concluded, although *Five Days One Summer* does give the Swiss Alps some minimal presence and dignity, and *Black Robe* gives a sense of the mixedwood forests of the Canadian Shield country.

I often find it hard to simply watch movies that contain natural landscapes, particularly period pieces, because I am looking for evidence of disturbance or inconsistency. In *A River Runs Through It*, I spent the whole time watching the foreground and background vegetation, looking for diffuse knapweed or forest clearcuts, both of which are dirt-common in modern-day Montana, but which would have been inappropriate to the early 1900s setting of the movie. Remarkably, I didn't see either, which meant someone associated with the film's production knew enough, and cared enough, to avoid them. In *Romancing the Stone*, the entire film is supposed to be set in South America but for some reason, one scene is filmed in a pasture that looks suspiciously like it is in rural Marin County.

My scientific experiment was further compromised by having to belatedly create an additional category called "pastoral," referring to movies set in rural areas that have achieved some esthetic balance between agriculture and natural landscape. This category contains some very fine works, of which I think *The Field* is the most significant, showing the absolute devotion to land that can develop in some rural societies.

The 1978 film *Days of Heaven* also deserves special mention. Cinematographer Nestor Almendros created an epic visual poem of the prairies and wheatfields of southern Alberta in this production. Throughout the movie, Almendros's lens keeps leaving the foreground action to reach out and caress the vast horizontal landscapes and thunderheads around Lethbridge. Or it will leave the action altogether to follow a coyote, horses running across prairie, or hunting dogs stalking a pheasant. The great critic Stanley Kaufmann maintained that this film proved his thesis that visual beauty is now a given in films, but beauty alone isn't enough to carry a film.

Other entries in the pastoral category are *Akira Kurosawa's Dreams*, the remarkable *Jean de Florette* and its sequel *Manon of the Spring*, *Stacking*, and *The Milagro Beanfield War*. This latter film contains shots of the exquisite high elevation pinyon pine/grassland association around Truchas, New Mexico.

The shadow of the western movie looms over this whole discussion. The western was a major genre in the movie industry right from its jerky, honky-tonk beginnings in *The Great Train Robbery* (1903) until it died somewhere around *Tom Horn* (1980), and every last one of these films contains sequences that were shot in natural landscapes. Yet a review of three above-average western efforts, *The Searchers*, *The Misfits*, and *Jeremiah Johnson*, confirmed my suspicions: westerns use natural landscapes as mere backdrops. The sagebrush and rimrocks and forests may as well have been painted sets. *The Searchers* (1956) was filmed in the spectacular Monument Valley of Utah, and the ranch house sets were built right at the base of some of the most awe-inspiring landforms on earth. Yet never once do John Wayne or the other protagonists comment on the landscape, or make any indication that their lives are affected by it. Other than the occasional use of landforms to make the chase sequences more interesting, *The Searchers* could have been filmed in a studio. Even two "modern" westerns, *Silverado* (1985) and *The Unforgiven* (1992), make no more than token reference to the landscapes they are set in. The modest resuscitation of the corpse of the western genre that is occurring right now has more to do with the American fascination with guns than it does with any interest in natural landscapes.

A few recent movies have taken the opposite approach of the western and consciously refer to natural landscapes with a kind of muddy, symbolic profundity. Several times in *Thelma and Louise* for example, the camera quite consciously leaves the faces of Geena Davis and Susan Sarandon to give us shots of a mute desert landscape (I think it's the Monument Valley again!). Using various natural landscapes as indicators of the psychological state of the human protagonists seems to be a legitimate cinematic technique, but this movie offers me no real connection between the actors and the landscape. I feel like director Ridley Scott is treating me to Symbolism 101, trotting out geological Rorschachs and encouraging me to guess at what they mean, when the reality is that the landscape shots are meaningless throwaways, with no real connection to the movie or the script. It is immoral to cinematically milk the awe inspired by dramatic landscapes without doing anything with them thematically, but I don't suppose such a statement will ever find its way into Hollywood's code of ethics.

Jane Campion's recent film *The Piano* makes more credible connections between landscapes and the psychological state of the characters. Most of the film is shot in dense, oppressive New Zealand jungle, except for an outstanding scene shot on an empty ocean beach (empty, that is, except for a piano). We are made to feel the contrast between the dark, claustrophobic jungle settlement and the unrestrained freedom and openness of the beach. The differing characters of the two men in the film, Harvey Keitel and Sam Neill, are underscored by the settings of their homes. Neill is a "colonist" in the true sense; he is busy clearing and surveying his land, and his house is surrounded by burnt trees and thick mud. Harvey Keitel, on the other hand, has "gone native" and his house is surrounded by pristine jungle.

A very arbitrary choice of the top five movies that contain plot-connected natural landscapes would be *The Treasure of the Sierra Madre, The Field, Fitzcarraldo, Days of Heaven* and *The Milagro Beanfield War.* The choice is arbitrary because my null hypothesis was not disproven: none of these or any of the other films I have seen really meet the criterion I set out. Painting and still photography contain hundreds of classic representations of nature, but the great natural landscape feature film is yet to be made. The medium of the motion picture is closest to what the human eye actually perceives, but for some reason, we are more compelled by the static and abstracted *images* of landscape that painting and still photography offer, as opposed to the truer *representations* of landscape seen in films.

It would be unfortunate if film relegated itself to the kind of quick-hit, instant-overload style so popular in advertisements and music videos. Film *is* effective with these rushing, hyperkinetic and superficial montages, but it can also be effective as a medium for depth, fascination, and obsession. Bits and pieces of the movies referenced here are ample proof of that. There is much more to landscape than the purely visible, and film — the ultimate visual art — can demonstrate that.

Movies are about escape. They provide a window through which we can climb out of our own lives and daily situations, if only for 90 minutes at a time (although 180 and 270 are options). The standard apertures for these escapes — glamor, horror, sex, action, suspense and violence — are fine as far as they go, although I question most of the violence. But an unfulfilled need remains, an unopened window. I want to be invited in to someone else's landscape visions, to scan their darkling plains instead of my own, to let them control the field glasses.

Scientists, even gentleman scientists, are bound by the great tradition of their craft to say very little at the conclusion of their experiments. As Bertolt Brecht has Galileo say:

> We crawl by inches. What we find today we wipe from the blackboard tomorrow and reject it — unless it shows up again the day after tomorrow. And if we find anything that would suit us, that thing we will eye with particular distrust.

Already I have made claims that are not supported by data, claims that Galileo would have rejected. This is an ongoing problem that forever condemns me to gentleman scientist status. Perhaps here is the very stuff of the first true landscape film: the clash between the scientific and the artistic approach to nature; a battle of wills, a western of ideas. If this movie were ever to be made though, I would have a problem deciding who rode the black horse, and who rode the white.

⊙

16

Homage to Jane

LANDSCAPE IS NATURE'S ENTERPRISE. In doing her business, nature employs capital and assets in worldwide operations that humble the biggest multinational, and she does it without, as we must remind ourselves, any need for human intervention. Our modest, fumbling equivalent to nature's landscape, our greatest common enterprise, is the city.

Saskatoon is one of those fumbling equivalents, a young city built on the prairies of Saskatchewan. Not long after Saskatoon was founded, the province's university was too and, typical of most universities in Western Canada, it was built outside of the city, and Saskatoon eventually grew out to surround and absorb it. As a graduate student there in the 1970s, I lived for a time in the small village of Sutherland, just beyond the campus, and normally walked to the University every day through the agricultural research fields. For a few days every winter the temperature on those windswept fields would get so desperately cold that even my full-length, down-filled, tube-hooded Hudson's Bay coat could not keep me warm. Outlaw wind, straight off the northern tundra, would instantly erase my footsteps in the dry snow, and then reach right into my thighs to grip the muscles in ominous embrace. On those days I would take the city bus home. In those days, Saskatoon had not yet made formal links with the village of Sutherland, but anastomosis had already occurred, by way of the bus system.

It happened that Percy Wright got on the same bus I did, on one of those short, brutal February afternoons. Not many old men got on the bus at the university, so I took note of this individual. He wore a kind of formal black coat with a velvet collar, a fur hat, and galoshes. His hawk nose was accentuated by cheeks slightly hollowed by age. His glasses were the old-fashioned bifocals and he had a stubbly grey moustache. Sitting down across the aisle from me, he pulled off his mittens, and extracted a small glass vial from one as he did so. I watched him as he turned the vial about in his hand, looking at it speculatively. I was pretty sure it wasn't a prescription.

"What've you got there?" I finally asked, intrigued by this Victorian-looking gentleman on the Number Seven bus as it made its way through arctic wastes to Sutherland. The old man answered with the name of a chemical that to this day I can't remember.

"What's it for?" I persisted, counting on the patience of the aged.

"It's one of the drugs the Faculty of Medicine is testing to overcome the rejection of human organ transplants." He paused. "I am going to try it on a particularly difficult tree graft."

I got off at his stop, which turned out to be a few blocks from mine, and followed him home, like a puppydog.

He told me his name was Percy Wright: he had started out wheat farming north of Saskatoon, but by the fifties he had gradually converted the farm over to a nursery and greenhouse operation, a rarity on the Canadian prairies in those days, until age drove him off the land, and into the village of Sutherland. He made this transition well, picking an old house with a big yard in that prairie village-turning-suburb, and promptly filled the yard with the rare birds of northern prairie horticulture — pears, oaks, true apples, roses. And he began to graft, scion to seed stock.

Percy invited me in and his wife made tea for us, while she gently scolded her husband for not taking a cab on such a cold day. We soon became kindred spirits, Percy and me, sharing common interests in plant lore and other obscure subjects.

Cities, for all their corrosive and monstrous qualities, contain layer upon layer of fascination for me. Here is an ecology we ourselves have built, with scapes of our own making, upon which we now play out much of the surprise and disappointment of human experience. I am amazed at how we can produce such ugliness together with such rare beauty in cities — how chance encounters with visionary old horticulturists can co-exist with needle exchanges and drive-by shootings.

For years I felt furtive and guilty about my interest in cities, and I think I can trace that furtiveness back to one period in my life. When I was thirteen we moved from a small town to Seattle, Washington. To get home from school I had to take a bus downtown and then transfer to another one. I lied to my parents about how long the trip took, and every afternoon I would get off in the unknown world of Seattle's downtown, my transfer safely in my pocket, to go exploring. I learned everything: Skid Row, the waterfront, Pioneer Square, the library, First Avenue, and multi-ethnic Jackson Street. Then there was Ben Paris, a basement emporium off Pike Street that fascinated me, a kind of male holdover from the 1930s that contained sporting goods, barbershops, cigarstores, perimutuel betting, a tavern, restaurant, shoeshines, newsstands, and a Western Union office. What else could be found along those dark and smoky corridors I could only guess. I found that by walking about the place briskly, as if I were on an errand, I could avoid getting thrown out. Certain other downtown places would also tolerate a boy's presence, like second-hand bookstores and stamp shops, where I could look at the merchandise and observe the mysterious grown-up world around me, without being asked to leave. I memorized the bus schedule and kept close watch on my Timex, so as not to blow my cover.

This interest in cities remained furtive well into adulthood, and I was often less than totally candid with myself and others about why I needed to travel to a particular city. Part of my re-exploration was to come clean about my desire to visit cities occasionally, and to understand some of the motives behind that desire.

There is a continuum in the way we see things, one that reaches from untouched wilderness all the way through to the most intimate and artificial of all scapes — the insides of our own houses. This river of perception springs from sources in the natural landscape, and then flows farther and farther into explicitly human territory, as it moves through landscapes modified by agriculture and forestry, to gardening, to landscape architecture, through urban planning and finally, to interior design. As an ecologist trained in the art of finding patterns in the natural landscape, it is understandable that I am drawn to the most densely and explicitly patterned of our human landscapes, the downtown areas of cities.

The experience of say, walking a quiet Nelson alley at night, as a heavy winter snowfall settles upon it, should be fundamentally different from a natural landscape experience, but there are similarities. Outlines of buildings bordering the alley loom in complex, velvet-black arrangements. Seen from up close, the back walls of the buildings are naked of ornamentation and pretense, and reveal a hundred-year span of construction materials. A modern sports car, illuminated from above by a 1920s incandescent streetlight, is slowly being buried in falling snow. Spidery, black-iron fire escapes climb upward, out of the dim pools of streetlight, upward into the void. A grimy dumpster with empty lettuce cartons stacked beside it looks oddly refined and well proportioned. My eyes are continuously challenged to perceive and interpret patterns. If I try new sight angles, the elements of this alley come together into ensembles I had never thought of before. Light and dark, shape and pattern. A nighttime grove of western red cedar along a creek, with the odd scrap of moonlight reaching the ground here and there, would be a totally different environment than the alley, but it would surely engage some of the same engines of perception, some of the same faculties of analysis and pleasure.

Should urban landscape patterns be immediately obvious and visible to us, since we ourselves created them? I don't think so. The patterns are not all that simple, perhaps because some of what we build and do in cities is not conscious but instinctive and biophysical, like the cedar forest is.

The North American experience is now primarily an urban one. I think it is worthwhile to look at this artificial/biophysical enterprise — the city — with the same faculties and attention that we normally save for natural landscapes. Jane Jacobs, whose seminal book *The Death and Life of Great American Cities* stood classical urban planning on its ear, did some of that looking at cities and identified four factors that made them vibrant, innovative and safe:

- High *concentrations* of people (as opposed to large *numbers* of people).
- Different primary uses intermingled, such as residences and work places.
- Small, short city blocks.
- Buildings of different ages, types and conditions of upkeep mingled together.

Jacob's statements, written in 1961, bear uncanny similarity to today's principles of landscape ecology. High biological diversity ("biodiversity") is a primary goal of any ecosystem. As the number of separate species within an area increases, more niches are occupied, more food chains are established, nutrients and energy begin to flow between various life-forms, waste products are recycled and the ecosystem becomes dynamically stable, better able to adapt to change. Cities display the same phenomenon. Ethnically and occupationally diverse communities are effective generators of business innovation, and are better equipped to survive economic downturns, just as diverse ecosystems are better able to handle disturbance. Cities whose districts cannot be neatly classified into Commercial, Office, Residential, Industrial, and Warehouse tend to be more successful than those with clearly separated districts.

Jacobs makes an interesting comparison between two cities in England during the 1850s, at the height of the Industrial Revolution. Manchester, with its massive textile mills and planned neighborhoods, was the "model city," where everything was geared to smooth, efficient textile production and distribution. Birmingham, on the other hand, was outside the main transportation network, had a hodge-podge of neighbor-hoods, and a whole series of small, messy industries that kept changing. Makers of gun barrels, for instance, would switch over to manufacturing the new metal nibs for fountain pens. Other companies would suddenly shift their production from a product to improved versions of the tools and dies that they had been using to produce the product. As time went on, Birmingham evolved into a great city, and Manchester slipped into economic oblivion.

Natural ecosystems reject the "efficiency" of a thousand acres planted to a single crop in favor of a variety of species assemblages; cities that reject the single-industry economy in favor of business diversity are always better off in the long run. Edges between natural ecosystems are always ragged and interpenetrating; large areas committed to a single use or to a single species are more vulnerable to damage than many small, distinct areas mingled together. Silviculturists, who tradition-ally managed forests on an "even-aged" basis, are now switching to "uneven-aged management," which encourages the presence of juvenile, mature and decadent trees in the same area. Perhaps some day we will see the link between old-growth and old houses.

The strong similarity of principles between natural ecology and Jacobs' urban ecology is no fluke. Any biological system operating in time and space will eventually attempt to follow ecological principles, even when that system is made up of alienated, techno-driven, hyperconsuming urban men and women, who are biological only when their deodorant fails.

Jane Jacobs took on the dominant Le Corbusier school of urban planning, the nightmare vision (which most of our cities still try to follow) of gleaming office towers, consumer malls and sprawling, monotonous suburbs, all connected by high-speed automotive throughways. She said the model was all wrong, and in its place she offered pure funk; short blocks, decreased reliance on the private automobile, pedestrian dominance, and small business. The essential enterprise of a city, she said, is the creation of new and innovative products and services, and that creativity requires a unique, messy, even inefficient urban environment:

The conditions that promote development [of new goods and services] and the conditions that promote efficient production and distribution of already existing goods and services are not only different, but in most ways they are diametrically opposed.

Funk runs counter to everything developers and planners believe in, but funk works. A few cities are recognizing the validity of this and other Jacobs findings, thirty-five years later. A few are also beginning to realize that, as more and more nature disappears into the maws of urban development, the loss must be replaced by architecture, plantings, art and social spaces that mirror, in some derivative way, what we look for and need in nature.

The perceptual continuum from raw nature to the living-room has the potential for human bonding at each point along it, so long as the modifications we contemplate are sustainable, retain a sense of humility relative to the natural landscape base, and reflect human dignity. Most of our attempts at the built environment fail to meet these criteria. I make occasional visits to cities like Vancouver, Toronto and Seattle, and as I travel their freeways, those cancerous and metastasizing neurons of concrete, and through the distorted commerce and housing that follows them, I find myself asking, from the perspective of the most privileged age and society in history, "is this the best we can do?" Of course not. In the end I retreat gratefully back to my own small town of Nelson, whose built environment is still human scale, and whose natural landscapes are still within reach.

Landscape provides habitat, and habitat is the ground of experience. We humans are unique in being able to create bad habitat for ourselves and, in doing so, we contribute to the making of negative personal and social experience. The downtown office highrise habitat is a good example. It violates all of Jacobs' four criteria (including the high concentrations of people principle, since those concentrations are only there for 40 hours out of every 168). The highrise environment has uniform, hard edges, something rarely seen in nature; it cannot be modified, and cannot evolve. As a landscape, its natural equivalent would have to be the sterile stonefields of Baffin

Island, where the only evidence of life lies buried underground, in paleontological strata.

Another bastard landscape is the standard exurban commercial strip road. This is the four-lane thoroughfare that is packed with car lots, drive-through banks, fast-food restaurants, shopping malls and gas bars, the same strip that has gutted most of the downtowns of North America. To truly appreciate the noxiousness of the strip, it is necessary to walk one, preferably on a Friday or Saturday night. The strip has removed all reference to nature, and then further enclosed all the human references behind neon signs and automobiles. Nothing is left for the pedestrian but a vacuum of exhaust fumes.

Small parts of the urban landscape are devoted to parks and ornamental gardens, in conscious imitation of the natural landscape. Often these spaces are neither good people spaces nor good natural spaces. The formal geometry of squares, rectangles and circles seen in parks denies both the natural and human tendencies for skewing, unequal clustering, and imbalance. How many times have I walked along the rectilinear concrete pathways of some city park and seen the deviant but graceful shortcut veering off, where unsanctioned footsteps have worn a more functional trail across the grass? Architecture and planning are nearly always formal, but use is nearly always informal. The mixture of mowed grass, individual trees and massed flowerbeds so common to city parks and managed landscapes has a very distant origin in those forest edge environments that were the cradle of our species, but those environments were anything but rectilinear, and the grass didn't get mowed.

Parks are important to the spiritual life of a city, but the open spaces available just outside of a city are equally important. Fingers of seminatural landscape should reach into the edges of a city, leading outward to the larger natural body. This allows the urbanite to maintain a more balanced perspective. The architect Christopher Alexander, in his book *A Pattern Language*, suggests that cities limit their size and develop in an interlaced pattern of "city-country fingers" so that no one in the city is more than a twenty-minute walk away from open space.

Emerson, Thoreau and Whitman are all known for their writings about nature, and yet we need to remind ourselves that all three of these men were essentially city dwellers. The cities they lived in though, were unique. Concord and Brooklyn in the mid-1800s were cosmopolitan and intellectually stimulating communities, but whenever Ralph, Henry or Walt felt the urge, they could hike the twenty minutes to the edge of their town to commune with a natural landscape, or perhaps just walk off a hangover (well, Henry or Walt, anyway). These men were Romantics: they saw a positive fusion of humankind with nature, partly because their home towns were at that time cosmopolitan, compact and adjacent to significant areas of natural landscape, and no doubt had city/country fingers as well. The writing of these three has endured, partly because of the native talent they possessed, and partly because the ambience they lived in — small, vibrant cities surrounded by agrarian and natural landscapes — is a particularly satisfying and productive human habitat.

Many forces operate against this kind of urban/agrarian/natural landscape complex. Because we have located so many of our cities on level, fertile land, we not only lose farmland to city encroachment, we lose most nearby natural landscapes as well, since they will be converted to agriculture. It is easy to think of the city as monster, devouring everything, eating its own young. Conventional planning wisdom has it that larger populations create greater demands for goods and services, thus stimulating economic growth. This theory of unlimited growth, as Edward Abbey points out, is the ideology of cancer.

Backyards may be the only bright spots of the urban green space. The front yards of most houses usually follow the typical park pattern of squares of grass and circles of flowers, but occasionally a backyard will allow a more informal meeting of nature and culture. Here, sagging fences mingle with rampant quackgrass, clotheslines with gardens and swing sets with staggy old fruit trees. The result is often comic, but hopeful. The very occasional person may even make a unique landscaping statement in his or her front yard. There is such a house and yard on Richards Street in downtown Vancouver, sandwiched between the featureless BMW repair shops and advertising agencies that characterize that part of the city. The house is festooned with flowerpots and handpainted signs, and any space in the tiny yard not occupied by a lawn ornament is gardened within an inch of its life. The place has a look of cheerful senility about it, a to-hell-with-resale-value look, one that must drive the BMW owners and ad execs crazy. In the Richards Street context of business hustle and aggressive conformity, it is a staggering statement of individuality and a willingness to publicly display one's personal esthetics. As soon as I saw the house, I knew immediately that an eccentric old couple lived inside, and that I wanted to be just like them when *I* got old.

Artificial landscaping must go one of two very divergent ways: either it references and harmonizes with natural landscape, or it must be consciously and flamboyantly "artificial," declaring whimsy, as in the house on Richards Street, or reflection, as in a Japanese garden, or some other purely human emotion.

The city, like nature, has ecotypes, separate areas that can be defined by their form and function. The common is one of these ecotypes. The common is an ancient concept whose only modern equivalent is the downtown city park, a piece of free, open ground within the city where people can publicly interact, play chess, stroll, make speeches, do pantomime, agitate, meditate, and so on. Along with the freedom to do what one wanted in the common came the responsibility to preserve and maintain the opportunity for others to do the same thing. If there is to be an urban equivalent to the climax, old-growth landscape, the common would be it.[1]

The Tenderloin is another ecotype, the part of a city where any reference to natural landscape is formally abandoned, furtiveness is raised to the level of obsession, and all attention is focused on the ambiguities of gender, the human body, and the endless compulsions of the male sex.

The ultimate, final meeting of nature and culture is the urban cemetery, and landscaping that echoes the natural landscape is perhaps more important here than anywhere else. Cemetery visitors need the connected and oceanic feeling that natural landscapes provide; they need to sense the great ecological circle of birth, life, death, decomposition and finally, renewal into new life.

There is a tendency among some ecologists and environmentalists to automatically denigrate all human disturbance, and by extension, human works. I firmly believe there are some human changes to the face of nature that can be ecologically legitimate. Rejecting a role for ourselves is a rejection of our perfectibility, and a philosophy no less criminal than one that rejects the legitimacy of nature. This is a statement of faith rather than fact, but I believe that we as a species, together with some (not all) of our baggage and works, *can* create a valid niche in nature, even though we may not actually belong to it. I generally try to remind myself of this as I mentally prepare to visit a large city. Large cities, after all, are paradoxically the centers for ecological restoration. The urban experience somehow permits the kind of fierce devotion and fundamental impracticality — the random acts of kindness — that ecological restoration demands. Someday, those cities may be able to challenge the conventional wisdom. We all agree that exposing oneself to pristine nature is good for the psyche; someday urbanists may be able to point out the psychic value of exposing oneself to high-seral downtown city culture.

We are curious about other people, what they think, what they eat, what their fascinations are, how they look at their prime, and how they look at their worst. We are also amazed, and curious, about the things other people do in groups that they won't do alone. We engage in passionate searches for obscure and encoded information (an evening in any large metropolitan library will confirm that) and we need to expose ourselves to a certain level of random encounter. Cities exist basically to provide this randomness for us, and to satisfy our curiosity. There are layer upon layer of stories locked away in city sidewalks, stories that can satisfy this curiosity. Percy Wright's life was one of them. A city has to be generous enough, and the sidewalks wide enough, and the curiosity just deep enough, for the stories to be unlocked and told.

Percy is dead now, but at least one hybrid Canadian rose

and several northern tree-fruit varieties carry the tag *wrightii*. I don't think that chemical ever worked on any of his horticultural grafts, but the tiny vial in Percy's ancient hands on the Number Seven bus to Sutherland is symbolic of what a good city must do; provide an appropriate landscape for the infinite curiosity, and infinite diversity, of the human animal.

---

1. A distinction has to be made here between the urban "common" and the exurban "commons," that is, unowned or publicly-owned land that was used for communal grazing. Because no one took responsibility for the landscape, commons everywhere became highly degraded.

17

Ethics of the Plateau

MY RE-EXPLORATIONS were nearing completion. I had some business in Victoria, and found a company that flew between there and Seattle using small floatplanes. As I was about to clamber aboard the single-engine Otter, the pilot handed me a set of earplugs. I looked at him in mild surprise, and he pointed to the massive single engine ahead of the cockpit. "Can get a little noisy," he said.

We were soon up over Puget Sound, and I was grateful for the earplugs. The pilot didn't head directly north across the Strait of Juan de Fuca as I had expected, but instead headed westward, hugging the coast of the Olympic Peninsula. I supposed this was to minimize the airtime over the open waters of the Strait. We were flying low — only a few thousand feet — and I began to recognize old landmarks: Port Townsend, Discovery Bay, and then Sequim Bay. I realized we would be passing directly over Dungeness, where I had spent part of my youth. I pressed my face right up against the plexiglass window in anticipation; I had not seen the area for many years. The woods and coastlines of Dungeness were not primal landscapes for me, because I was already twelve by the time we moved there, but they were close. Soon I made out Dungeness Spit, an ancient, fishhook-shaped dune that extended far out into the strait. Inland from the spit was the broad floodplain of the Dungeness river, and then the great, upswept buttress of the Olympic Mountains.

Somewhere down below me would be our old house and Sherman's river pasture, but that was not what called my attention. Nor was it the Dungeness lighthouse or the memory of the old Haida war canoes half-buried in the sand at the end of the spit. It was instead the slopes of the Olympics, and the huge network of cutover forest land and ragged logging roads that ran halfway up the northern face of the range, and then stretched westward past Port Angeles on towards Forks, Sekiu, and Cape Flattery.

I sat in stunned silence. There was complicity here, I realized, as I reviewed our life in Dungeness in the late fifties; all of my friends' fathers, except for the odd farmer and teacher, were loggers, log truck drivers, or sawmill workers. Logging was what the two neighboring communities of Sequim and Dungeness did, and thought they did well. In fact, we honored the enterprise of logging every summer in a festival. Huge cedar logs would be buried upright in the schoolyard for the climbing and topping competitions. A twisting, timed racecourse would be laid out for log trucks in the school parking lot using eggs as course markers — axle-width plus six inches on either side. My girlfriend's father always won the driving events. Log rolling — already a heritage activity in those days — would be done in the sorting pond at the mill. The festival encapsulated the excitement and challenge of the rest of the year. Our fathers cut, and hustled, and drove, while we boys tried to make them proud playing football or basketball. It was a great life in Sequim and Dungeness, and no one had the slightest inkling that it could not go on forever.

The pilot finally banked northward and we headed across the strait to Victoria. I had no further desire to fly over these landscapes of my childhood, and sank back into the seat and into the powerful, soothing drone of the Otter's engine.

I seem to be standing now on a plateau, have taken up residence on it, in fact. The skies are clear but the wind is sharp, faintly alien, and the sight of the great distances is not a comfort. There, drifting in the remotest parts of the horizon's bluish haze, is the farther edge of the plateau, the break in the curve of resources. I don't want to be here. I want to be back in that earlier Olympic rainforest where one day I slipped and fell off a rocky outcrop and was saved from injury by landing armpit-deep in a fallen, rotted cedar. Those were mountain-sides of abundance and this plateau is eroded. The wind carries with it a whiff of apocalypse.

I can see prospects from this plateau that were simply not visible to anyone in the 1950s, in Dungeness or anywhere else in North America. I can now examine the trajectories of our resource use and resource degradation — agriculture, mining, forestry, urban land use, commercial fishing, energy and a dozen others — and project those trajectories forward to the point where I can see the farther edge of the plateau, the dramatic break in the resource curve. The coming break may be thirty years distant for some resources, perhaps fifty or a hundred and fifty for others, but each falldown is now out there, in the future, well within our comprehension, waiting for us to intersect with it. The overcutting of the forests of the Olympic Peninsula, or the crash of the Newfoundland cod stocks are early, prophetic examples of these falldowns.

Standing on the plateau gives me a curious sensation, probably something like what my parents felt when I was twenty, when tie-dyed shirts were emblems, the Vietnam War was in full swing, and a protest march or sit-in had either just happened or was about to. My friends and I simply knew the times were a'changin, but my parents and the rest we gleefully called "The Establishment" felt that the very pillars of western civilization were being shaken. Now it is *my* turn to feel that same mortal fear, not because of the younger generation, apparently content to follow in our footsteps, but because of *us*, because of our inability to look across the plateau and confront the future.

In spite of the widespread co-opting and trivialization of the term, *sustainability* is the issue here. Can we arrive at a level of natural resource consumption that just equals the natural rate of replenishment of those resources, and can we arrive at a level of global pollution that just equals the earth's ability to absorb and neutralize those pollutants? Can we factor in an appropriate rate of technological innovation that reduces waste and that generally makes life more intelligent rather than more absurd? Can we sustain ourselves long enough to sort out our relationship with nature and find a useful middle ground between science and the mystical?

The word sustainability seems to be used in radically different ways, and it is amazing how often one sees the word in the same breath as the word *children*. Environmentalists block logging trucks because they believe forests are an essential part of the biosphere, on which their children depend, and that current logging practice is not *sustainable*. Loggers, on the other hand, march on government buildings because they fear restrictions on logging will make their children's lifestyles *unsustainable*. Same term, diametric opinions.

Implicit in the concept of sustainability is *carrying capacity*, a term that comes originally from the humble discipline of range management. Finding carrying capacity in range terms involved three steps: first the manager had to determine how much grass was produced in a below-average growing season. Then he or she worked out how much grass the wildlife needed, plus how much should be left untouched for the grass to restore or sustain itself. What was left over could then be allocated to the economic activity of livestock grazing. The concept of carrying capacity has gradually worked its way into wildlife biology and now is beginning to be heard even in urban planning circles. Managing populations so they stay in long-term balance with the resources of their habitat is a clear, homespun, and powerful idea, an idea endorsed by nature.

My youth in Dungeness was punctuated by football games and there was a particular one I played at Forks, very near the northwestern corner of continental United States, that stands out in memory. Our schoolbus arrived at the town of Forks, perched on a steep, forested hillside above the straits. The Forks team, mainly Indian boys, met us in the school parking lot. There was no football field in sight, and no room for one, either. The Forks team got on the bus with us and we drove ten minutes up a logging road, through Olympic rainforest, to get to a level bench where the football field was. When the bus stopped, I got out slowly, dumbfounded: there lay the one hundred yards by forty alright, but it was surrounded by the biggest cedar trees I had ever seen. A wisp of fog hung in the air a few feet above the fifty-yard line, and there was silence everywhere, except for the drip of the trees from a recent rain. I walked out on the field: it was not grass, but a thick layer of soft, resilient cedar bark. There were no change rooms, no grandstands, no cheerleaders, no soft drink concessions.

It was a transcendental game: soaring, twisting, sinuous, quiet. We all became like deer, exempt from score. Our coach was mystified.

Could we have been sustainable in Dungeness, lived within our carrying capacity and still had all that fun? I have no proof, but I have a gut feeling that the difference between unsustainable and sustainable consumption might turn out to be precisely the same difference between our current childish extravagance and reasonable, creative, satisfying use.

The steady roar of the Otter's radial engine reminded me that these landscape insights over Dungeness came courtesy of a very energy-intensive technology. Our consumption of energy, particularly of fossil fuel energy, is a good issue to test against the ethic of sustainability. With oil, we seem to have found the ultimate free lunch, at which we have been gorging steadily for a hundred years now. We are in absolutely no danger of running out soon, and any momentary hiccup of price or supply is usually followed by a quick expansion of proven reserves. But we can't make fossil fuel, alternatives like solar power and gasohol seem to be mere blips on the horizon, and in that hundred years we have gorged on an abundance that accumulated over a million years. However, it seems in the nature of things that no natural resource is unlimited, and overconsumption will generate problems long before the resource actually runs out.

In the early eighties I worked for the Office of Energy Conservation in Saskatchewan, and had the opportunity to present some information on fuel-efficient tractors to our boss, the Minister of Energy, himself a grain farmer from Moose Jaw. The minister listened politely until I was finished, and then launched into a description of the two monster four-wheel drive tractors he owned, one of which burned *ten* gallons of fuel per hour, and then there was the bigger, which burned *fifteen*. As he talked, I slowly began to realize he was not expressing concern, but was actually bragging about his two behemoth machines. Something, some funny feeling about this man, told me not to argue with him. The minister, who was known to use a riding snowblower to clear his front and back yard every time it snowed, obviously considered us a nest of radicals and closed the office shortly after that conversation. He also went on to murder his wife, who probably did argue with him.

Rampant consumption of fossil fuel is now absolutely central to North American life. We flirted with high prices during the seventies, and while most people accepted conservation — some enthusiastically, some grudgingly, and others, like the Energy Minister, not at all — business decided it was not good for us. Unlike Pinocchio, we got the chance to go back to Pleasure Island a second time, back to childish extravagance. Now we have built that energy extravagance into every aspect of our society. E.F. Schumacher once said that if Martians examined the British biscuit industry, they would become convinced that biscuits must be loaded onto trucks and driven several hundred kilometres before they became edible.

I think if I were allowed a single, magical master-stroke, one that would most improve sustainability and our relation to the earth, I would increase the price of fossil fuel. This would rationalize agriculture; suddenly it would make sense for Manitobans to grow their own carrots and Montanans to grow their own lettuce instead of trucking those commodities in from California and Mexico. Suburban and rural smallholdings, currently stagnating in either marginality or decadence, could suddenly regain small-scale productive purpose again. And perhaps I could no longer stand by the side of the highway at the top of Stagleap Pass, one of the highest passes in Canada, and watch loaded logging trucks grinding up over the mountain, *going in both directions*. The Winnebago subculture might even disappear, providing great material for future archeologists. Suddenly it would be less compelling to consume agricultural land and commit ourselves to even more freeways and traffic by building big-city suburbs. Suddenly urban mass transit would become attractive and fiscally healthy; suddenly the automotive output of smog and green-house gases would slow its precipitous increase. Intelligent regional cultures might even begin to emerge, as people would remain connected to the larger world but discover what it means to belong to a place. We might even find time for the spiritual within the context of North American life.

The energy crisis of the seventies showed us that fossil fuel consumption is price-driven, and my master-stroke of increasing price would produce a nicely predictable decrease in consumption and increased interest in alternatives. But my master-stroke for resource sustainability is encrusted with ethical dilemmas. If the price of fuel goes up, who gets the extra money? The Seven Sisters of world petroleum would love to have it, but they would have done nothing to earn it, and would not be likely to plow it into new technologies for further reducing consumption. If, on the other hand, the price increase came in the form of a government conservation tax, then a great number of things could be done. Roads and highways could become completely self-financing. Mass transit could be further subsidized. Funds could be channelled into automobile exhaust pollution control and research. Taxes could be rebated to the petroleum industry to beef up oil tanker safety and reduce oil spills. In other words, conservation taxes could serve not only to reduce consumption in specific natural resource extraction sectors, but could also provide self-financing for conservation research and pollution abatement in that same sector.

Logical, sensible plan, the sixties part of me says, remembering the days when governments were not walking conundrums. But the other voice, jaded with contemporary experience, says no. Why? Massive, uncontrolled bureaucracies. Arrogance of governmental power. Empire building and loss of purpose. Regulations to control the dishonest 5 per cent that stifle the other 95 per cent. The economic distortions of subsidy. The gullibility of government funding agencies in the face of research hustlers and tax credit artists. We ask governments to impose restraint and resource ethics on us in lieu of doing it ourselves, and then complain bitterly about their failings. Perhaps it is just as well that I don't get my one chance at a master stroke. I would probably hesitate at the last moment.

Just before the Otter touched down in Victoria's Inner Harbor, I looked back toward Dungeness. The white, sandy bluffs of the coastline were unnaturally elongated by the mirage effect created by the sun's heat radiating off the water of the strait. I remembered how that same mirage effect colored my images of Victoria, as an impressionable youth in Dungeness. I had never been to that city, and it was in the mysterious country of Canada, so I was free to turn those wavering heat mirages into the delicate white minarets of an imagined, exotic metropolis. Victoria is now an experienced and rather ordinary reality, but now I found myself wishing imagination and mirages could transform the clearcuts of the Olympic mountains back to a semblance of the cedar forests they had once been. Clearcuts no larger than football fields, perhaps.

The farther edge of the resource plateau is the one landscape that I have no interest in exploring. A question hangs in the air above it: why, having seen the edge of this plateau, do we still consume natural resources at the current level of extravagance? Whether we consider our kind as part of or separate from nature, it is time to decide whether our species is here for a good time, or a long time.

◉

18

The Logistics of Epiphany

I WENT BACK TO THE KOKANEE RIDGE once more, in the final coil of my spiral of re-exploration. Like the criminal who returns to skulk, I wanted to see the amphitheatre of my first emotional passage again. This time I got to the trailhead early in the morning, and felt none of the urgency on the switchbacks that had been so strong on the first trip. The hike to the saddle seemed remarkably easy this time; distance on a known trail always seems to be shorter than on an unknown one. A young couple with heavy backpacks and a dog passed me, and we chatted briefly. The dog, in the true fashion of the Kootenays, was a mutt wearing a red bandanna. As I walked on, I realized I had not seen anyone on the previous trip. As pleasant as the couple was, they did not figure in to my plans for the day. As Max Oelschlager says, the wilderness experience is essentially a selfish one, and we all prefer not to encounter strangers on the trail. Humans are great consumers, and to individually conquer and occupy new territories is the greatest shopping binge of all.

When I reached the saddle I took a small side trail that headed away from the lake and up on to the Kokanee Ridge itself. The trail soon disappeared as I entered a massive rockfield, but the ridge was in plain sight above me, so I started through the rocks, looking up now and then to check my bearing. The shattered granite, detritus from the ridge above me, ranged from Volkswagen size on down, and was piled randomly in a layer twenty feet thick. Slushy ice still lay in the protected spots, and in places I could hear water running underneath the rocks. My ankles suddenly seemed fragile and unprotected, and I picked my way carefully, testing each rock before stepping on it. I felt like an ant crawling across a shag carpet: forward movement could only be achieved by an endless series of ups and downs. However beautiful the whole ridge complex was, this particular rockfield was not people-friendly. I think I tend to operate under the assumption that the Earth is basically designed for me, and I often react with mild surprise when I encounter violent weather, a host of hungry blackflies, or a field of sharp, delicately balanced rocks.

The rockfield finally thinned back to bedrock and I stopped to rest. Looking down on the jumble I had just come through, I suddenly saw its logic; it was the belly of this concave mountainside of granite, a horizontal band where the shattering ridge rock found its angle of repose.

The re-exploration had taught me that natural landscapes attract me because they are, simply, in order. Just like this rockfield, they possess a complex, complete and self-organized existence that is totally independent of us. Even the chaotic new landscapes created by receding glaciers possess a logic of their own. The change and evolution produced from an order may be rapid, uneven or incredibly slow, but a landscape knows its way and progression just as surely as spawning salmon know home water. Landscape orders are uneven, multidimensional continua that will contain significant elements of chaos; if we perceive them to be fixed points, it is from a failure of understanding, and imagination. They are beyond our understanding of purpose.

I had also learned that natural landscapes are infinitely more complex than any facet of human life, and that our competitive nature is not content with the idea of complete, independent entities that stand apart from us. The separate order goads some to modify, others to dissect and research, still others to destroy. (How many suburban shopping malls ultimately owe their existence to this frustration, to the unknowability of nature?) In the end though, the complex, unknowable order of natural landscapes, their independence from us, and their sheer physical beauty, remain. Perhaps only as a symbolic memory, like the plains buffalo.

The last leg up was a scramble on the chunky bedrock, following the sides of rock funnels and ending on the narrow ridge itself. There was a delightful sense of arrival, and I shared a moment with sister peaks that rose above cloudy valleys and common piedmont, a sorority linked in majestic line of sight from Alaska to Mexico. The ridge itself was just a few feet wide. On its far side lay a small glacier. The Purcells were in plain view and, beyond them, the higher peaks of the Rockies. Then I turned back to look down the way I had come and saw the saddle and the little alpine lake, the site of my first epiphany.

It is part of my nature and training to be suspicious of spiritual, untestable experience, but that event and others that had followed could not be denied. Those experiences had revealed to me one hidden basis for my natural landscape compulsion, a bit of natural truth, one that stitches this mountain and a thousand other landscapes together. Natural landscapes do attract the nonrational side of my human nature, and give me leave for spirituality. I had established this basic commonality alright, but more than that, I had opened an unexpected window, letting in brief and unexpected gusts of vastness, of landscape-level emotion. These landscapes, these spiritual nunataks, had an independent, buzzing complexity, an elaborateness completely beyond the boundaries of my skin.

Acknowledging the spiritual was a difficult bit of truth for a nonreligious skeptic, one who does not feel particularly moved by any of the New Age persuasions. But I do take it as given that many, perhaps most of us, do search for personal epiphanies, these curious events of joy and transcendence. Epiphany has its sources in religion, but now I had seen secular flows, on mountain saddles, in sagebrush and along forgotten rivers. Mysticism, transcendence, ritual, ecstasy, redemption; this is not a catalogue of strictly religious properties, rather it is one of fundamental human needs. If I can generalize at all on these intensely private quests for secular epiphany, the experience of natural landscapes, and perhaps of a certain kind of sexual intimacy, are its truest sources.

I put my pack down on the ridge and found a comfortable, sun-warmed rock to rest against. As I looked across the endless serried rows of mountains, the Canadian painter Lawren Harris's canvases came to mind, as if a mental curator had unexpectedly brought them out from storage. I realized immediately that Harris too would have had his cry in the mountains, trembling at the passage of monstrous and unexpected emotion. That experience was now obvious as I thought about his landscapes. The paintings are strongly simplified, showing what he called "a change in the outward aspect," with detail replaced by essence. Sky and brooding mountain are often joined together by shafts of binding light. The viewer's perspective is usually detached and at some altitude above the ground, as if from a promontory or even a glider. Typical Harris subjects were those extreme environments of the Rockies, the Arctic and the Canadian Shield where vegetation is minimal and landscapes are profoundly simple. In his best works, he participated in the great natural rituals of light and illumination. Lawren Harris understood the landscape view of things, but even more importantly, he painted the connection between landscape and spirituality.

By the time Harris began painting mountains like the Kokanee Ridge, he was a master at managing the logistics of epiphany. In the 1920s, he and fellow painters Lismer and MacDonald fitted out an old boxcar with food, bedding and supplies, and would hitch it to Algoma Central trains heading into the shield country of northern Ontario. When they judged the shapes and colors of sky and landscape they were passing through to be sufficiently new and different, they would ask the engineer to drop their boxcar on some lonesome siding, and then paint for a week. They even brought along a hand-driven pushcart "speeder" to give them more mobility up and down the rail line.

Harris and the rest of the painters of the Group of Seven jointly redefined the view of the Canadian landscape, freeing it from the oppressive influence of European tradition, but

Harris took his painting a step beyond the rest. For a time he adopted Theosophy, a curious blend of Eastern religion and color theory. He, more than any of the others in the group, seemed to be drawn to the spiritual aspects of landscape, and sought "to become one with ever purer means of expression." Harris sought that oneness more than most, and his search was not without some pain.

My re-exploration had taught me some modest logistics for my own craft. Observe, and harvest the observations; writing, in my own case. When life rises above the mundane, as it does occasionally, damn the embarrassment, observe passionately, and harvest immediately. Pay equal attention to lore, science and spirituality. Talk to visionaries. Restore an eroded gully. Understand the genius of the horned toad. Design a landscape ritual that your mother would be willing to participate in. Learn geology.

I climbed down off the ridge slowly, through the rockfield and back onto the saddle, this time stopping at the little promontory where I had camped before, to take a last look. The saddle was there for me, not waiting, not subservient, but enduring and accepting. In spite of the casualness of that first trip, the saddle, these parallel ridges and this pure, alpine lake had revealed themselves to me as the realms of another kingdom. It is here then, precisely here, on remembered and future landscapes, on Manitoba prairie, Washington scabland or Colombian high plateau, that I may be allowed to bend the given and rigid line of reality ever so slightly. I have the great and rare privilege to change nature's outward aspect, and to be changed by it. Tawny mountain peaks can now swell up to magic fortresses along the frontiers of my vision. Venus and the moon can veer from millennial orbits to conjoin for me in this amphitheatre, and I am allowed to connect. Permitted to join reason with spirit, and given leave for epiphany.

⊙

Bibliography

1. THE MOUNTAIN ELECTRIC

Affleck, Ted. *Kootenay Yesterdays.* Vancouver: Alexander Nicholls Press, 1976.

Agee, James. *Let Us Now Praise Famous Men.* Boston: Houghton Mifflin, 1980.

Pielou, E.C. *After the Ice Age.* Chicago: University of Chicago Press, 1991.

3. VISIONS OF SCABLAND

Allen, John and Burns, Marjorie. *Cataclysms on the Columbia.* Portland: Timber Press, 1986.

Baker, Victor, ed. *Catastrophic Flooding: The Origin of the Channeled Scabland.* Stroudsburg, Penn.: Dowden, Hutchinson and Ross, 1981. (Contains most of Bretz's key papers; currently out of print.)

Eaton, Diane and Urbanek, Sheila. *Paul Kane's Great Nor'West.* Vancouver: University of British Columbia Press, 1995.

4. FOSSICKING ON THE BORDER

Keast Lord, John. *The Naturalist in British Columbia.* Vols. I & II. London: Richard Bentley, 1866.

MacLean, Norman. *A River Runs Through It and Other Stories.* Chicago: University of Chicago Press, 1976.

Stegner, Wallace. *Wolf Willow.* New York: Viking Press, 1962.

5. COWBOY FICTION

Bell, William. *Will James, The Life and Works of a Lone Cowboy.* Flagstaff, Ariz.: Northland Press, 1987.

Bramlett, Jim. *Ride for the High Points: The Real Story of Will James.* Missoula: Mountain Press, 1987.

James, Will. *Smoky.* New York: Scribners, 1926.

James, Will. *Lone Cowboy: My Life Story.* New York: Scribners, 1930.

6. CYCLES OF FIRE

Covington, Wallace and Moore, Margaret. "Southwestern Ponderosa Forest Structure: Changes Since Euro-American Settlement." *Journal of Forestry* Vol. 92, No. 1 (Jan. 1994).

Kay, Charles, et al. *Assessment of Long-term Terrestrial Ecosystem States and Processes in Banff National Park and the Central Canadian Rockies.* Banff, Alta.: Parks Canada, 1994.

Kaiser, Leo and Knuth, Priscilla, eds. "From Ithaca to Clatsop Plains: Miss Ketcham's Journal of Travel." *Oregon Historical Quarterly* No. 62 (1961).

Murphy, Alexandra. *Graced by Pines.* Missoula: Mountain Press, 1994.

Pyne, Stephen. *World Fire.* New York: Henry Holt & Co., 1995.

7. PRIMAL

Van Doren, Mark, ed. *The Portable Walt Whitman.* New York: Viking, 1945.

9. THE IMAGE AND THE BREAKS

Lionni, Leo. *Parallel Botany.* New York: Knopf, 1977.

10. TALLGRASS DREAM

Baldwin, A.D. Jr., ed. *Beyond Preservation: Restoring and Inventing Landscapes.* Minneapolis: University of Minnesota Press, 1986. (Contains Jordan essay.)

Butler, William. *The Great Lone Land: A Tale of Travel in the Northwest of America.* Toronto: Musson, 1924.

Epp, Henry. *Three Hundred Prairie Years: Henry Kelsey's "Inland Country of Good Report."* Regina, Sask.: Canadian Plains Research Centre, 1993.

Mills, Stephanie. *In Service of the Wild: Restoring and Rehabilitating Damaged Land.* Boston: Beacon Press, 1995.

Morgan, John et al. *Restoring Canada's Prairies.* Winnipeg: Manitoba Naturalists Soc., 1995.

12. HIGH DESERT

Hunt, C.B. *Physiography of the United States.* W.H. Freeman and Co., 1967.

Cohen, Leonard. *Selected Poems, 1956-1968.* Toronto: McClelland, 1968.

Miller R.F. and Wigand, P.E. "Holocene Changes in Semiarid Pinyon-Juniper Woodlands." *BioScience* Vol. 44, No. 7 (1994): 465-474.

13. MEDITERRANEAN

Stebbins, R.C. *A Field Guide to Western Reptiles and Amphibians.* Boston: Houghton Mifflin, 1985.

14. THE NATURE OF NATURAL

Dr. Seuss. "The Lorax" in *Six by Seuss.* New York: Random House, 1991.

Eiseley, Loren. "The Star Thrower." New York: Times Books, 1978.

15. ON SUSPECT TERRAIN

Brecht, Bertolt. *Galileo.* New York: Grove Press, 1966.

Kauffmann, Stanley. *Before My Eyes: Film Criticism and Comment.* New York: Da Capo, 1974.

16. HOMAGE TO JANE

Alexander, Christopher. *A Pattern Language*. Oxford: Oxford University Press, 1977.

Jacobs, Jane. *The Death and Life of Great American Cities*. New York: Random House, 1961.

Jacobs, Jane. *The Economy of Cities*. New York: Vintage Books, 1970.

17. ETHICS OF THE PLATEAU

Everett, Richard. *The Eastside Forest Ecosystem Health Assessment*. Vol. 1, Executive Summary. Wenatchee: USDA, Forest Service, 1993.

Schumacher, E.F. *Small is Beautiful: Economics as if People Mattered*. New York: Harper and Row, 1973.

18. THE LOGISTICS OF EPIPHANY

Oelschlager, Max. *The Idea of Wilderness*. New Haven, 1991.

New Society Publishers focuses much of its publishing program on tools for developing sustainability in a number of different spheres. If you have enjoyed this book, you may also want to check out the following titles:

- *Our Ecological Footprint: Reducing Human Impact on the Earth,* **by Mathis Wackernagel & William Rees.** Presents an exciting and powerful tool for measuring and visualizing the resources required to sustain our households, communities, regions and nations into the future. (Ninth in *The New Catalyst's* Bioregional Series of books, all of which deal with aspects of sustainability.)
6" x 9". 176 pages.
Canada Pb: $17.95. ISBN: 1-55092-251-3
U.S.A. Pb: $14.95. ISBN: 0-86571- 312-X

- *Simplicity: Notes, Stories & Exercises for Developing Unimaginable Wealth,* **by Mark A. Burch.** Mark eloquently explores voluntary simplicity as a means to personal sustainability, sketching a practical, enriching alternative to the culture of consumption, as well as paths you can take to joyously change your life.
6" x 9". 144 pages.
Canada Pb: $15.95. ISBN: 1-55092-269-6
U.S.A. Pb: $12.95. ISBN: 0-86571-323-5

- *Whose Common Future? Reclaiming the Commons,* **by The Ecologist Magazine.** Tracing the world's environmental crisis to the dismantling of the commons world-wide, *The Ecologist Magazine* analyses the forces behind the destruction of commons regimes, and highlights effective strategies for protecting and recovering them.
5½" x 8¾". 224 pages.
Canada Pb: $17.95. ISBN: 1-55092-221-1
U.S.A. Pb: $14.95. ISBN: 0-86571-277-8

- *Home! A Bioregional Reader,* **edited by Van Andruss, Christopher Plant, Judith Plant, and Eleanor Wright.** More than 40 contributors make this a compelling introduction to the classic thought and literature of bioregionalism — the exciting movement for (re-)creating an ecological, sustainable society rooted in community and a culture of place.
8½" x 11". 192 pages.
Canada Pb: $19.95. ISBN: 1-55092-007-3
U.S.A. Pb: $16.95. ISBN: 0-86571-188-7

- **Full Catalogue on the Web**: http://www.swifty.com/nsp/

- **Toll-free ordering number** (VISA & MC only): 1-800-567-6772.

Don Gayton

A scientist and range ecologist by training, Don Gayton's writing has appeared in numerous magazines and journals in both Canada and the United States, including *Harrowsmith* and *Equinox*. His first book, *The Wheatgrass Mechanism* (Fifth House) was based on over 15 years experience of living and working on the Canadian prairies, winning the Saskatchewan Writers Guild Non-Fiction Award for 1988. Don's in-depth experience of the natural landscapes of western North America has been filled out by a wide variety of unusual jobs which include his being a community developer in Latin America, a hired man on an Okanagan cattle ranch, an agricultural extension agent on Saskatchewan Indian reserves, and a steelyard worker. He lives in Nelson, British Columbia.